Perhaps one  my own hid to other me. One such event is etched in my memory, a heartfelt discussion with an inmate named Harvey…

It had been a tough conversation as we sat in the visiting area of the institution. He was back inside for a revocation after doing so well. He was staying clean, studying at university, reconnecting with friends and family. Then it all fell apart. The loneliness started to build. It was too much. Next came a friendly welcoming group, a beer, and then the downward slide began.

As we sat looking at each other, talking about his attempts to somehow give back, make atonement for the horrible things he had done, we talked about the burden we both carried, the reality that nothing brings back the dead. There is no way to fix it. We just need to learn to live with it.

I looked at him and just made a statement of fact. I didn't know it would hit so deep. "Harvey, you're a good man. Your heart longs to make amends. You are a good man."

The tears slowly slid down his face, a face etched with years of journeying through gangs and death.

We sat in quietness. My heart ached to give a magic moment of healing. I had none. All I had to offer was to be present, encouraging him as he wrestled to find the path that would help him heal, and learn to live with the reality of the void he had left in the lives of others…

A Lifer's Journey

Prison Chaplaincy
from the Inside Out

Hank Dixon

Prairie Heart Press
Winnipeg, MB

Published June 2021 by Prairie Heart Press, an imprint of Story
Perfect Inc.

Prairie Heart Press
PO Box 51053 Tyndall Park
Winnipeg, Manitoba R2X 3B0
Canada

Visit http://www.prairieheartpress.com for more Canadian prairie
books.

Dedicated
to
Linda

I was drawn to the Light
which sought me out.
I handed my life
into His great care,
with prophets and apostles,
echoing through time,
"All will be well, if you rest in His call."

I could not foresee
the gift He would give.
Her eyes sparkled and danced,
the first day we met.
Her gentle grace,
quietly touching,
my hardened shell.
A whisper of Wind spoke softly to tell,
"This is the one you dreamed of in a cell."

Faithfully you walk
close by my side,
through valleys and hills,
with your love and light.
As we grow old,
together as one,
a whisper of Wind, speaks softly to tell,
"This is the one you dreamed of in a cell."

Contents

Introduction

Those who bear the mark of pain
are never really free.
They owe a debt to the ones who still suffer.
This is your beginning...
(Author Unknown)

The Place of Reckoning

I did not want to go back to prison. That wasn't my plan. I hated the place. Yet here I was, wrestling with exactly that pull. A light wind caressed the surface of the lake, creating a gentle rhythm of water lapping up against the grey, pocketed chunk of granite on which I sat.

My perch rose about four feet up from the shore, half in water, half on the beach. Its rounded shape revealed it to be a souvenir of the last Ice Age, discarded at the edge of this body of water known as Little Tupper Lake. The boulder sat at the end of a short path, a ten-minute walk from the parsonage in North Brookfield, Nova Scotia, where I had pastored for the last six years. My trips to this ancient rock were becoming more frequent as I wrestled, argued, and battled with my God. The world outside was quiet and serene. The world within was in turmoil. I was losing the battle.

The struggle began months earlier through a series of events that culminated in a visit with a special friend, Sr. Teresa Currie. Our daughter Teresa is named after her, a measure of her impact on my life. Sister T, as she was known, could be—well, to be nice about it—a stubborn, persistent firebrand, all wrapped up in a deeply caring prison chaplain who loved to spoil her namesake. Years before, she had abandoned the confines of a habit and cloistered living to minister to men in prison.

As we were about to leave her house, Sister T looked at me. "Hank, have you ever considered prison chaplaincy?"

I was taken aback. She had stepped into a sensitive place in my life. Others had ventured there and were met with an angry rebuttal. After serving nine years in prison, the last place I wanted to be was back inside.

My resistance to returning grew out of two reasons. First, bad things happened there. I simply did not want to go back. Second, I knew that my past, in certain circumstances, could be my greatest deficit inside the wall. I always felt those who were so certain I would be successful back inside had never read Jesus' comments on the subject. After a visit to his hometown, He remarked, "A prophet is not without honour except in his own town." (Mark 6:4)

This time, though, as I stood in the doorway of Sister T's house, surprise shifted to confusion. No anger rose up. Her eyes told me she was asking because she truly believed this might be God's calling on my life.

I fumbled to find an answer. "I'll think about it," I finally said.

That became my problem. I did think about it, and the more I thought about it, the more her words worked their way into the deep spaces of my heart, merging with God's voice calling me back in.

So, there I sat, on my perch before the lake, my place of reckoning. The future I had so carefully planned out was brought to a sudden halt as this persistent, troubling call refused to leave. The prophet Jonah and I could have kept each other good company. I knew which direction his situation had gone. Fortunately for me, Little Tupper Lake was not the domain of big fish. I tried to muster excuses, only to be reminded that Moses used the same lines. I also knew where that situation had gone. Perhaps most troubling, were Jesus' words to Peter after he was given his calling: "I tell you the truth, when you were younger you dressed yourself and went where you wanted; but when you are old you will stretch out your hands, and someone else will dress you and lead you where you do not want to go." (John 21:18)

Those words struck at the core of my rebellious spirit, even though I'd known from the beginning that my walk with the Lord would entail sacrifices and challenges. After being released from prison I met my beautiful wife, Linda. We were married in 1987. I pursued further education: a Bachelor of Arts, Master of Divinity, Internship as a Baptist minister, Ordination with the Canadian Baptists of Atlantic Canada. I was determined to follow through on the call God had placed on my life. There had been many difficulties to get to this point. Like many other pastoral couples, Linda and I sacrificed a great deal to pursue the call into ministry.

But this call to go back inside was more than I had bargained for. It was too much to ask. So, I fought and argued, until this one fateful evening, as I sat on that ancient rock mulling over my options for escape, when a confrontation with my conscience pierced home:

Hank, how can you say no to the One who restored your life from the dark pit you drove it into?

There was silence within. I stared out at the creation around me, warm clouds drifting through the sky, casting shadows over a soft wind-swept lake. I wept. I had lost the battle. I was going back to prison.

The Journey Inside

It had been fourteen years since I left prison. I remember the day well. It was July 4th, 1985. Sister T agreed to drive me to the halfway house in Halifax. On my way up to the main entrance, I stopped by Admission and Discharge to pick up what few belongings were still in my personal effects from 1976. With a single box in hand, wearing an ill-fitted pair of dress pants and an out-of-date sports jacket that draped over my shoulders like a worn rug, I moved through the main entrance, barriers and gates slamming shut behind me. I must have been quite the sight. I didn't care. I was getting out of prison.

The day was a flurry of activity, but one moment is stamped in my memory. As I stood at the main entrance waiting for Sister T to arrive, the officer behind the desk looked me up and down. With a distinctly condescending tone he growled, "You'll be back."

No doubt he had seen his fair share of men return to prison, or maybe he was just in a bad mood. I remained silent, keeping my anger in check.

The officer was right. I did come back. He would not be the last prophet in blue I would meet.

I was a reluctant prison chaplain. Even as I submitted my application for a position, then went through the vetting process and interview, I hoped it would all end.

It didn't. In the fall of 1999, I entered prison chaplaincy with the greatest of trepidation. Of all places to start, I found myself in a federal maximum-security institution ready to blow. I arrived in September of 1999. In January of 2000, Atlantic Institution in New Brunswick was rocked by two major riots back-to-back—more about that later.

Despite the fears, apprehension, and resistance to going

back in, I spent fifteen years working inside: four years at Atlantic Institution and eleven years at Stony Mountain Institution in Manitoba. What held me—what compelled me—to work in this environment turned out to be something that overpowered all the fears and concerns I had walking in. What developed was a deep well of compassion and care for inmates and staff that has never left me.

Another Calling

In 2013, federal prison chaplaincy in Canada was thrust into a significant change regarding the way chaplains were engaged to serve in prisons. For over twenty years individual clergy could apply for positions. After a vetting and decision-making process, the faith tradition to which you belonged would be offered a contract to provide services at the institution. You would then be employed and paid by your religious authority (denomination) via the contract.

The system had a few problems that were becoming increasingly difficult to surmount. The government of the day eventually decided to shift from multiple contracts with individual faith-based groups to a single contractor model for providing chaplaincy services across the country.

For those of us who had years of working in the federal prison system, the single contractor model presented a potential problem. Powered by the wrong motives, a single contractor model could result in poor quality chaplaincy services. For instance, should an organization with no understanding of federal chaplaincy take on the contract, or whose bottom line was to make a profit, services would suffer, and so would chaplains. As a result of numerous conversations around this issue, Kairos

Pneuma Chaplaincy (KPCI) was formed by a group of chaplains and a former Associate Director of Chaplaincy. It was incorporated in May of 2013 and won its first contract in November of 2013.

The central purposes of the organization were to try and maintain the professionalism, interfaith nature, and supportive structure that existed for individual chaplains in Canadian federal prison chaplaincy and try to improve these elements.

For two years KPCI provided good quality federal prison chaplaincy services across Canada. During that time, I left my position as a chaplain at Stony Mountain Institution and took on the role of Regional Manager Chaplaincy Services on the Prairies for KPCI. I also completed my Doctor of Ministry degree in 2014 and turned my attention to designing workshops for chaplains, along with developing an undergraduate prison chaplaincy course for Booth University College.

In 2015, KPCI bid on the next contract but lost to another organization. The criterion for awarding the contract was simple: the lowest bidder. In April of 2016, the new contractor took over providing federal prison chaplaincy services.

As the new contractor began soliciting chaplains to work for them, I chose not to apply. After nine years of serving time, fifteen years of working through riots, disturbances, murders, and suicides as a chaplain, and two years of supervising chaplains, it was time for a break. Along with leaving chaplaincy, I also decided not to continue teaching chaplaincy courses at Booth University College. My new position as Program Director at Open Circle, a prison visitation program based in Winnipeg, Manitoba, required a large time investment.

I planned to walk away from prison chaplaincy and offer no further commentary. That proved to be more difficult than I anticipated.

With the reality of a second contractor taking over the

federal chaplaincy contract, some chaplains began to feel uncertain about their future and chose to exit federal prison chaplaincy, seeking more stable employment opportunities elsewhere. As the exodus continued, a wealth of wisdom and experience began leaving the federal prison system.

In observing these changes, I grew concerned. A vacuum was forming, one in which new chaplains entering prison chaplaincy were given little training regarding the theology, philosophy, and practice of prison chaplaincy. Added to this, the structures that had been in place to provide mentorship to new chaplains were disappearing.

Over the years, friends, colleagues, and acquaintances occasionally asked when I would share my story in print. I had always deflected such suggestions. There are others who have written prison conversion stories. There are any number to choose from.

Now, though, I was starting to see how years of serving time as an inmate had provided a unique view on chaplaincy that might prove helpful to others. I had more to tell than a prison conversion story.

I began to think, is it time to write?

As I reflected on putting my story and personal reflections into such a public arena, another place of reckoning began to emerge. I had shared small portions of my journeying in various settings. However, there were experiences I had not shared with anyone, or only with a few close friends. Some of those would need to be part of the story. Added to this dilemma, was the concern about drawing others into my story because, of course, they are part of my experience.

As I attempted to move the most difficult experiences to paper, I would encounter a wall of resistance. Prayer and struggle ensued as I was left staring at an empty computer screen. In one of those moments, I penned the following:

I wonder who built this wall? Is it there to protect me or a barrier to be dismantled? If it is for my protection, what is it protecting me from? Maybe it is just a mirror, reflecting back my own fears. On the other hand, maybe it is crafted from common sense, a barrier to save me from myself, from drowning in the emotions and darkness of a prison world that lives in my memory. One that plays out each day in the lives of those who are still inside.

So, I sit here, staring at the wall. Every once in a while my hand moves through it to jot down a few words, some thoughts, a story, a reflection. Then the pressure builds. It is almost painful. My chest throbs, my head aches, my arm grows weak and I pull back to the safe side of the wall.

I am left with a dilemma—who is pushing me to pierce the wall, God or man?

I am still not sure I have a good answer to that question. I suspect time will provide it. Perhaps my call is simply to step out in faith and share.

As I learned many years ago, sitting on a rock overlooking Little Tupper Lake, God does not always provide us with a clear vision of what lays ahead. Our calling, at least mine, has always been to trust and follow Him.

1. Darkness and Light

The cords of death entangled me,
the anguish of the grave came upon me;
I was overcome by trouble and sorrow.
Then I called on the name of the Lord:
"O Lord save me!"
(Psalm 116: 3-4)

Jack London, one of the great writers of the last century declared, "The most beautiful stories always start with wreckage."

That is where this story begins.

Confusion

Every morning was the same. I awoke to find steel bars flooding my view. Eight feet away stretched a catwalk covered in thick steel mesh fencing which ran the length of the range. On the other side of it were windows with more steel bars. Beyond, a blue sky, clouds drifting freely by, mocking me as I gazed out at them: *Take a good look, loser. Any freedom you had is long gone.*

It wasn't a dream. I was in prison. It is hard to describe. You go to sleep hoping to escape the dismal world you find yourself in. You awake, jolted back to reality. Whatever dreams of freedom you may have wandered into during the night are swiftly shattered by the reality that surrounds you—a small rectangular box of steel and concrete, a dark depressing cage.

Slowly my mind began to orient to the world on the inside. It didn't look any better than the day before.

One morning, as the cell doors were unlocked, I pulled on my pants and wandered out onto the range. It was quiet this time of the day. Breakfast was an hour away. Most of the guys slept in. They had no interest in returning to the reality that would be theirs when they awoke.

I walked over to one of the steel tables on the range and plunked myself down. I gazed around the range, Observation Post on one end, cells down the length, showers at the other end, all of it dressed in a miserable grey paint that reflected my mood. I hated this place and my existence in it, the latter hate being particularly difficult to live with. There is nothing worse than realizing your life is a big mess and the only person to point a finger at is you.

Absorbed in my thoughts, I nearly missed the box sitting on one of the tables. Wondering what treasures might lie within it, I sauntered over to have a look: books, lots of them. That was a welcome surprise. I started sorting through them, pulling out a couple of Westerns. Then a title grabbed my attention: *The Late Great Planet Earth*, by Hal Lindsey.

Great, I thought. *Always enjoyed a good science fiction story.* Returning to my cell, I threw the books I had collected into a corner and pulled on a shirt. The call for breakfast came blaring through the speakers.

Laying back on my bunk later that afternoon, I opened the science fiction book for a good read. What a disappointment! It was a religious book, all about prophecies in the Bible and how the world was going to end.

I thought about chucking it aside, but something stirred within. I wondered, *What if there is some truth in this stuff?*

As a kid I went to Sunday school and church for a short time. I didn't learn much. I was an outcast in school, and it was no different in Sunday school. I once attended a church Bible Camp. That adventure cured me of any illusion about how loving church people are supposed to be. The teen counsellor assigned to our cabin was an angry, frustrated kid who took great pleasure in making my life miserable. I had little use for church, religion, or those who claimed to be saintly.

Still, something continued to stir, so I kept reading. As I finished the book, I came across a small section in the back that talked about a personal relationship with Jesus Christ. I wondered what that was all about.

The next day, while sitting on a steel table, still pondering Hal Lindsey's work of fiction, I spotted a Salvation Army Officer coming up the catwalk. I stopped him halfway down the range.

"Hey, man," I said. "I need to talk."

"What can I do for you, son?"

"Well, I just finished reading a book and I need to talk to someone about it."

He paused for a moment. "You know, I can send someone who could relate to you better than I can." And with that he was gone.

I was left wondering, *Who can relate to me?*

Geek Encounter

It didn't take long to find out. A few days later, a voice shouted from the control post, "Dixon! You have a visitor."

The visiting area for the maximum-security unit was right beside the range. A locked steel door provided access to the inmate side. A row of steel stools was anchored to the floor behind a plexiglass shield separating you from your visitor. Speaker holes were drilled through the shield. There was only enough space between the wall and the stools for you to walk in and take a seat.

When I stepped into the inmate side, I was surprised. Not just because my visitor was on the same side of the glass, but because of what I saw. A twenty-something-year-old stood in front of me. A bit overweight, he had a big grin on his face and wore a set of geeky horn-rimmed glasses. *Oh no,* I thought, *this is one of those religious holy rollers. It's written all over him. Probably a Christian camp counsellor at one point in his life. This is the guy who can relate to me?*

I stood there for a moment, pondering my options. He represented a number of things I disliked about so-called Christians. Clean-cut, with that pious happy air which sometimes turned out to be as phony as the values they claimed to live by.

That familiar feeling stirred again, and I sat down, guarded, unsure about whether I wanted to talk at all. I don't remember much about the conversation. He introduced himself as Greg and I think he asked about my life, my situation, what family I had. I don't remember my answers. In the end, he offered to come back and see me again. Then, he did the unexpected.

"Hank. Can I pray for you?" he asked.

I was dumbfounded. No one had ever prayed for me, at least not that I knew about.

"I guess so," I said.

"Well, let's pray together."

My gut reacted. I thought, *Are you nuts? I am not going to sit here surrounded by clear plexiglass which everyone can see through and pray with you!*

Gritting my teeth and trying to be as nice as possible, I said,

"Man, you go ahead and pray, but don't expect me to. It's not my thing."

While I sat there, feeling extremely uncomfortable, Greg, the holy roller, prayed.

We shook hands after, then I wandered back to my cell, never expecting to see him again.

The questions I sought answers to went unasked. The moment I'd laid eyes on him, I'd decided his answers were of no interest to me. They were going to be pat, simple, religious hocus pocus. I had heard enough of those over the years. How I wanted to get high and just find some way to shut off all the confusion, pain, and that overwhelmingly oppressive, numbing shame.

I had lived through a few lonely times in life, but when society—the world you lived in—looks at you like a piece of trash that should be hung from a length of rope until either your neck breaks, or you choke to death, you can't feel any more desolate than that. I was a nineteen-year-old drug addict, facing a second-degree murder charge. It had started as a break-and-enter to steal money. There wasn't supposed to be anyone in the building when we broke in, but there was. Quickly the night spiralled out of control, leaving a caretaker murdered.

Editorials clamoured for a return of the death penalty, which had been abolished in 1976, just months before my crime. TV, radio news, and talk shows echoed the same sentiment.

There were three of us on the range facing murder charges. We never spoke about the dark place we all occupied. It was better not to talk about it.

Darkness

Loneliness is a powerful force. It can forge unusual friendships.

Not long after our initial meeting, Greg returned. This time he had secured an office space to use. I learned he was a volunteer at the prison. Every couple of weeks we would meet to talk about any number of things—except religion, especially as it related to my personal life. I resisted any attempts by Greg to probe deeply.

His visits became a welcome diversion from the stress of dealing with all the other worries in my life. As a drug addict, I was used to dealing with problems by enveloping my life in the foggy haze of pills, grass, hash, or my favourite, speed.[1] Drugs, whatever your preference, have a wonderful way of quieting the internal turmoil. They either take you to another place, or dull the painful throbbing ache of living a loser's life.

Along with the inner garbage that made up my life, I was facing a life sentence in prison and had no idea when, or if, I would get out. There was no escaping the reality that I would be found guilty. I was not going to do time well. I hated being confined and often found myself daydreaming about being back in the world of my youth, camping in the woods of Northern Ontario, awed by the dancing Northern Lights, listening to the haunting call of a loon over a glass-still lake.

Suicide was an ever-present option. A plan was already in the works should things get really bad. I had timed the officers'[2] rounds at night and looked into some effective ways of doing it—

---

[1] Speed is a methamphetamine. It can be snorted, swallowed, or injected (sometimes called mainlining). The latter was my preferred method because it provided an instantaneous high.

[2] In recounting my experiences in prison, I have chosen not to use slang words such as "guard" or "screw" to define Correctional Officers. I have used these terms in the past as an inmate. I am no longer an inmate and have had the privilege of working with some outstanding officers. In my training with volunteers, I always encourage them to use the term "Correctional Officer". They are trained professionals and should be acknowledged as such.

either hanging, or slashing "up the arm" (not across). Apparently "up the arm" was a way to make sure you bled enough to die quickly. Of course, there was always the option of slicing your throat. One of the men on our range had a military background. He showed me to the right spot to cut. His mind was going to the same place as mine.

In the midst of it all, Greg kept coming back. While the rest of the world had written me off, he kept connecting. In my mind, that won him some credibility, even if he tended to spend too much time trying to talk about religious stuff. Occasionally it was irritating, but when you have a range full of guys, all awaiting trial in one form or another, all wrestling with their own personal garbage which occasionally spilled over into verbal or physical assaults, well, Greg's visits became a welcome reprieve—until one fateful afternoon.

After we began our usual conversation, something felt different. Greg appeared agitated, uncomfortable with the pat answers I was offering. Finally, he looked at me and said, "Hank, nothing is going to change in your life unless you let Jesus Christ in."

His words alone shouldn't have bothered me—this was just some religious guy trying to convert me. Even so, they sent panic and rage through my body. I could sense a presence enter the room. My whole body reacted. Somehow, I knew this presence and I didn't want to be around it. The longer I sat there, the stronger the presence became. I couldn't pin it down. This presence felt as if it wanted to get under my skin, deep inside me—like it knew me!

With rage rising within, I got up out of the chair and stared at Greg. "Get the hell out my life and don't come back." I walked out of the office.

A few minutes later, I stood at the barrier to the range. One of the new guys looked at me through the bars. "How did your visit with the holy roller go?"

As I stepped through the opening barrier, the dark twisted look on my face was enough to persuade him not to wait for a response. I went straight to my cell. That presence had rocked my world. I was angry, confused, and uncertain about what had happened. Not even a call for supper could move me from my cell. I longed for lockup so I could feel secure enough to go to sleep, my only escape from the screwed-up world I occupied. Although sleep came swiftly that night, it provided no escape.

I was never prone to nightmares. But what began to unfold in the deep of the night, in the dungeon of my mind, can only be described as terrifying. The landscape shifted and moved. The creature that gave chase changed forms as I sank deeper into a night of terror. At points the creature drew so close I could feel the heat of its breath on my back and hear a low eerie growl rise from its throat. The moment I looked back, my legs grew weak. It was huge, dark, with blazing eyes and a presence that spoke of one thing: destruction.

I couldn't shake it. No matter where I turned, where I hid, how hard I ran, it found me. It charged at me, chased me, saliva from its mouth dripping off its teeth, splattering on my heels. There was no escape, no place to hide.

Then, suddenly—a crashing sound! I bolted awake. Sweat covered my body. Slowly the bars came into focus, the thick steel mesh fence, windows with more bars, and a sky mocking me as I tried to push away the nightmare of the night and return to the nightmare of my day.

I sat up, staring out through the bars. Finally, I noticed the cell door was unlocked. Slowly I made my way on to the range, dazed, confused. The lingering images of the nightmare still haunted me.

I talked to no one. My mind was in free fall. I put off the

nightmare to stress, lack of drugs, whatever. As the day wore on, I hoped my escape into sleep later that evening would not see a return to that dark place. The lights from the security fence danced through the windows, distorted and twisted by those damned bars and the heavy fencing. I hated this place. I hated my life.

As the door clanged shut for evening lockup, I crawled back into bed, hoping sleep would come quickly. It did—too quickly.

With a fury that outstripped the first nightmare, it was back, more terrifying than the first night. All night long, I ran, I jumped, I cowered in small hiding places, only to feel that hot breath coming up behind me, huge jaws snapping at my back. At one point it snagged me, ripping into the shirt I wore. Exhausted, nearing the end of my strength, I awoke again to find myself in sweat-soaked sheets, breathing hard, not from physical exhaustion but from fear.

It took time to focus, to remember where I was. The nightmares were so vivid, so real. *What the heck is going on? Was it something I ate?*

I couldn't figure it out. This time I was determined to shove the dream and its grotesque images far from my mind. From morning until night, I engaged with those around me. I filled my waking moments with dumb conversations, card games that I was lousy at playing, even exercise on the weight machine. I must have been quite a sight at 6'1" and 160 lbs.

Lockup was called and everyone wandered back to their cells. I gazed down the range. In the last cell, one of the inmates, Tom, had his head stuck out, staring at me with a disturbing smirk on his face.

Fear rose from deep within. I was in trouble, way more trouble than facing a life sentence in prison.

As the officer moved down the range locking cell doors, I pulled my head in. The door slammed shut. My cell, with its locked steel door, was no longer a place that offered a measure of safety. Even here, in this locked cage, I was vulnerable.

As I sat on the bunk, pieces of the puzzle came together.

About a month earlier, while I was going out to talk to my holy roller friend, I also started talking to Tom. He was a Satanist and tried to persuade me that Satan could give me whatever I wanted in life, especially power. He even used the Bible as proof. "Hey, if Satan could offer Jesus all the kingdoms of the world, surely he can offer you the same. Or what about the fact that he is called the Prince of this world? He is the one who really controls this world. Satan even had the power to take on the Archangel Gabriel and hold him up from delivering a message. Imagine the kind of power Satan could give you."

His arguments were convincing, slowly drawing me in. Satanism was not new to me. Drug culture had its fair share of people who had encounters with the spiritual realm, both good and bad. I met a few over the years. Sometimes I engaged in long conversations with them, pondering what good and evil really were. I had also experimented with it.

On my sixteenth birthday, I went out with a group of friends to get drunk and high in a graveyard. It was secluded. No one went there at night. Through the haze of drugs and alcohol, I remember staggering away from the group with a bottle in hand. Finding a solitary place, I dropped to my knees and prayed that Satan would reveal himself.

I stayed there for a long time. The moment is anchored vividly in my memory. I remember kneeling in the soft well-kept grass, the smell of late-night dew, the gravestone in front of me, moonlight flickering off its granite face, how the pine trees rose on either side, as though gazing down at a confused kid who was so empty inside that looking for life in the darkness seemed a viable option. Nothing happened.

My thoughts were jolted back to the present when the catwalk gate slammed shut. The officers were doing rounds.

An unfamiliar feeling began to rise from within—desperation. It clawed at what little sanity I had left. I didn't want to go to sleep. I now knew what awaited me, not only another encounter with fear and terror, but something worse.

A couple of weeks earlier, Tom had explained the caveat for getting this power from Satan. I had to meet him. But no one could just meet Satan. They had to be prepared first. Tom explained the formula. Put a deck of cards under your pillow with one particular card facing up. That would be the signal for Satan to start sending nightmares your way. Each nightmare would get progressively worse, until you were desensitized enough to meet the Prince of Darkness.

After toying with the idea of trying it, I finally shoved the deck aside, thinking it was a bunch of bull. Yet here I was, facing night after night of nightmares. Unlike my night at the cemetery, something was now happening to me.

To make matters worse, it began to dawn on me I knew this phantom in my dreams. It had crept near to my life once before, the night of the murder. This same presence had been there, lingering at a distance like a grey cold mist off an ocean shore. Then I heard the shot. Swiftly, it surrounded me like a dark, condemning fog, my buried conscience whispering, *You've gone too far. There is no return.*

I sat staring at the concrete wall, tears welling up—not tears of remorse, tears of hopelessness. This was nothing like taunting evil in a graveyard. There was no life in darkness, just death. I was trapped.

Slowly, ever so slowly, the night moved on until I couldn't hold back the sleep anymore. I faded into darkness. There it was, hounding me, chasing, more vicious than the night before. I awoke with a start, yanked out of another hiding place, soaked, confused, feeling like I was going insane. Maybe I was.

I lost count of the days. Nothing seemed to matter anymore. All I wanted was an escape, some way out. This was destroying my life.

Suicide wasn't an option anymore. I knew what lay on the other side. I had met him.

Light

Somewhere in the maze of confusion, another presence emerged. It felt like a ghost. It said nothing. It never came close. It hung in the air for short periods of time, then it was gone. It almost felt like something gently whispering to me, not in words I could hear, but almost like a hand softly caressing me.

There were moments, as I sat on the range, staring out into space—grappling with the despair that comes with feeling utterly hopeless—when it would suddenly brush by, almost like it was beckoning me to follow, to listen, to see something where I saw nothing.

I wondered, *Is this what this Jesus thing is all about?*

Then I noticed something else. When this presence was around, the darkness was gone.

Somewhere in all the muddled thoughts and feelings, I began to realize that my only escape—my only way out—was to somehow, someway, let this other presence in. I had no idea how to do that.

Greg had talked about praying to let Jesus in. Where, how, and when was I supposed to do it?

This thought tumbled through my mind, one particular day, as I walked back into my cell for lockup. Now that I'd told Greg to never come back, there was no one to talk with. No one. As I flopped down on the hard bunk, I bounced between despair and a dim flicker of hope. The voices of men talking to each other drifted off into the distance as fatigue took over and I fell into a deep sleep.

Sunlight filtered through the bars and fencing as I woke. I sat bolt upright. *No nightmare!*

Quickly, I jumped out of bed. The cell doors had already been opened. Wandering out onto the range, I found it empty. As I leaned on the outside edge of the wire mesh catwalk, gazing out at the blue morning sky, I wondered what the day would hold.

Again, the dilemma of my situation began to sink in. A confusing array of thoughts and emotions started up. I couldn't even enjoy a beautiful sunlit morning without being pulled back into that turmoil.

Afternoon rolled around and the speaker announced, "Dixon. Someone here to see you!"

The officer led me up the stairs to the small office where I had always met Greg. There was lots of apprehension, as I realized it was probably him who had come to see me. Yet, strangely, there was also a sense of calm.

Greg had come back. He hadn't stayed away. After spending the morning in deep thought, I concluded his coming back, when I needed so desperately to talk, was no coincidence. I was deeply thankful.

I reached the doorway of the office. Resolve grew in my mind, the moment I saw Greg looking just as much the holy roller as the first time I met him, although now, there was apprehension written all over his face. I knew what I had to do.

I entered the office.

We looked at each other. The last time we met I left him looking hurt. I stood there for a moment, gathering courage.

"Greg," I said. "Don't say a word. I just want to let Jesus Christ into my life."

I wasn't sure what he thought. I didn't care. I dropped to the seat in front of him.

We bowed our heads and Greg led me through a prayer. I mumbled along, not even sure what I was saying. Jesus' name was in there somewhere, and the word "sinner" too.

My heart ached with a longing I had never felt before. An excruciating pain of loneliness rose from within. Slowly, gently, an overwhelming sense of the presence I had encountered on the range flowed over me. This time it was no ghost or fleeting whisper of wind. It filled the room, doing something I was unprepared for. It moved deep within me.

The ache and longing disappeared. The overpowering pain of loneliness melted away. In its place, something else began to grow, an understanding, a knowledge, an assurance that I belonged. I was no longer alone. I had a place in this vast cosmos. I was not a write off, a piece of garbage to be discarded and left to rot.

Wave after wave of this indescribable presence flowed through me. It was not like any high I had ever been on. This was different. It was grounded. I wasn't drifting off somewhere into a drug-induced fantasy world. Somehow, I knew this experience was solidly planted in reality.

"What is this, Greg? Why do I feel this way? What just happened?" I asked.

"You have given your life to Jesus Christ and as a result God has filled you with the Holy Spirit."

Over the next hour my holy roller friend tried to explain a number of things to me. I was too busy experiencing this new presence to hear much of what Greg said. The Holy Spirit and I were getting acquainted.

Challenge

Soon—too soon—it was time to return to the range. We parted, with Greg promising to come back and bring some study material.

The stairway up to the office was on the opposite range from the one I was housed on. That range had a different makeup than ours. It was filled with guys who had done federal time before. I came down the stairs and had to wait a few minutes before a door was opened to give access to my range.

As I stood there, close to the barrier, one of the guys from this other range came over to the bars. Looking me up and down, he said, "Hey, asshole. What are you smiling about?"

He was baiting me. He wanted me to walk over to the bars and confront him. Even though a barrier separated us, the gauntlet had been thrown down. I was expected to respond. When challenged in prison, you better step up.

All the guys on the range started gathering to watch what would happen. I stood there for a moment, looking at him. He was twice my size, just itching to harass this skinny kid in front of him. Any other time this would have escalated, skinny kid or not. Instead, a quiet calmness prevailed.

I said nothing. As he glared at me, the door finally opened and I left, walking through the corridor until I reached the barrier for my range.

I stepped back onto the range, unsure of what was going on with me. It was one thing to sit in an office, safe and comfortable, experiencing this new presence in my life. It was entirely different walking onto a prison range, with all its potentially volatile emotions. The doubts began surfacing. *Did something really happen to me or was it just my imagination at work?*

A couple of guys called me over to one of the cells. "Man, you look different. What happened to you?"

I couldn't help myself. I was so full of wonder about my encounter with Jesus Christ, I had to tell them.

"Guys, you will never believe what happened to me! Jesus Ch—" I didn't get further than that. Something like a bolt of electricity shot through my body, a nasty one. My tongue lost its strength. Rattled and confused, I quickly left, retreating to my cell.

Weird, unusual sensory experiences were not new to me. But this felt different. It felt holy, as if something or someone was trying to get my attention. I remember Greg talking about sin and the need to confess it. Maybe that's what happened.

I bowed my head. "Lord, I'm sorry. I didn't even know I was using your name in a bad way. Please forgive me." Instantly, a calmness settled within. I knew then, beyond any doubt, something dramatic had changed in my life.

The days and weeks that followed were so different from anything I had known in my past. I could not get enough of the Bible or the study booklets that Greg brought. Each morning, when there was silence on the range, I would sit and read, write, and pray, soaking up everything I could learn about this transformation I was undergoing.

Added to this, I simply could not shut up. Anyone who gave me the time would hear about Jesus Christ. There was only one problem: Tom.

A man I thought was a friend transformed into my enemy. The moment I began a conversation with someone about a religious topic, he was there, objecting to my viewpoints, insulting the Christian faith, calling down the religious people of the world. I could be standing at a cell door talking to someone and suddenly he would appear, curse words flying, as he attempted to provoke me. It got so bad I finally had to stop talking to the other guys on the range. It was a physical confrontation waiting to happen.

Bearing Light

A couple of months later I was convicted of second-degree murder with no eligibility for full parole for ten years.

Strangely, I was relieved. It was over.

My relief was short lived, though, quickly overshadowed by a deep apprehension about what lay ahead. Life with no parole eligibility for ten years. It seemed like an eternity to a twenty-year-old brain.

Greg continued to connect, assuring me he would come visit after I was transferred. The notice of my transfer was not long in coming. I was going to Prince Albert Penitentiary.

On a few occasions, I had tried to talk with Tom privately. Those moments were met with a hurl of insults and curses. I stopped trying, until my last night on the range.

Tom found himself in trouble and was charged with refusing to obey an order. Instead of sending him to the hole, staff gave him evening lockup. While the rest of us were out on the range, he was locked in his cell. Everyone avoided his cell, which was located near the end of the range. He could be miserable to deal with.

I walked down to the end of the range, Bible tract shoved in my back pocket (just in case), fully expecting to be met with a barrage of obscenities.

I stood at the bars for a moment. "Hi, Tom. I'm being transferred tomorrow. Thought I would just come to say goodbye." I braced myself for the verbal onslaught. Instead, I was met with a question.

"How are you doing?"

The deluge of hate I expected never arrived. For a moment I was speechless. Quickly, I recovered, and we spent the next hour talking about life, doing time, the future, our fears. He was afraid, very afraid. Tom was facing a first-degree murder charge, and nothing was going his way.

"Lockup!" bellowed down the range.

Quickly, I pulled the tract out of my pocket and handed it to him. Our eyes met. No words were exchanged, but he took the tract. As I turned to go to my cell, he said, "Thanks, Hank."

When my cell door slammed closed with that distinct metal-on-metal bang, I sat on the bunk, gazing through the cell bars, the steel mesh fencing covering the catwalk and the windows with more bars. It was dark outside, perimeter lighting casting a yellow glow over buildings and fences.

There were so many uncertainties ahead, but I was certain of one thing: I was different. Jesus Christ had entered my life. I wasn't sure what that really meant.

I found myself thinking about Tom and grateful the Light had found me in the darkest of places. But, I also hoped my talk with him had some impact. He would become the first person I added to my newly crafted prayer list.

2. Dark Night of the Soul

O Lord my God, I called to you for help
and you healed me.
O Lord you brought me up from the grave;
you spared me from going down into the pit.
(Psalm 30:2-3)

Entering Prince Albert Maximum Security Penitentiary, I was a man on fire for God, jumping into my newfound faith with an abandon that surprised even me. I walked away from drugs, studied Scripture at every opportunity, and prayed on a daily basis. I witnessed to anyone who would listen, which of course brought its fair share of mockery. None of it fazed me.

Eventually, I was able to secure a transfer to Springhill Medium Security Institution in Nova Scotia. I was looking forward to the freedom a medium environment would bring, with more opportunities to live out my faith.

Little did I know, it would not last…

Descent

I sat on a cold, concrete ledge outside Unit 9 at Springhill Institution, staring into the distance. It was a cool July morning, no wind, sun, or clouds. The yard was all but empty. A couple of guys wandered around, waiting for work to be called. There I was in my prison greens, dulled to anything in the world around me. With every minute, I grew more numb.

The call had arrived fifteen minutes earlier. I travelled down the range and walked into the office. I was given no explanation, just a phone receiver handed to me. On the other end was my mom. I don't remember much of what was said except, "Your father died last night."

It was a short conversation. I wasn't sure what to think, what to feel, what to do. How are you supposed to react to your dad's death?

As I walked back up to my cell, one of the other lifers on the range asked what was up. I mumbled something incoherent in reply.

I grabbed a jacket from my cell and headed out of the Unit, into the yard I now found myself in.

Am I supposed to cry? I thought. I sure as hell wasn't going to do that here. Besides, my feelings seemed more like a jumbled snake pit of conflicted emotional movement. I couldn't sort them out.

Suddenly, the Unit 9 door burst open and guys started wandering out. Once in a while someone would look at me, but no one spoke. Then Ben came out, walked over, and stood in front of me.

He lived just a few cells down from mine. Stocky, built like a tank, with a face chiselled in granite, he was the last person I would expect to say anything. In a thick Newfoundland accent, he uttered words that have been etched into my heart for over forty years: "Hey, Hank, heard about your dad dying. Really sorry to hear about that."

His eyes locked with mine for a moment, driving home the sincerity of his words. Somehow, he understood. As quickly as he arrived, he turned to go to work. In a world of concrete and steel where men don't share their pain, this tough burly Newfoundlander extended words of sincere compassion I have never forgotten.

It is hard to explain. It was a moment in time. I had no idea what I was feeling. I was stuck in this damn prison. I hated being here. Life was difficult and empty enough. It had just become emptier. Then, a few words of care, spoken in sincerity, in a place where there is precious little concern for another, by one who seemed to know what I was experiencing—it gave me a ray of hope.

In the days that followed, I met with the Chaplains. I didn't share much with them, not because there weren't things to share, but because I was a twenty-one-year-old "former" drug addict who had spent most of his life running from pain, burying it behind drugs.

I had no idea what I was feeling, until they told me I wasn't going to be allowed to attend the funeral. I was too much of a risk. Out of that jumbled snake pit one emotion roared to life. Anger...an anger that bordered on rage.

It is one of the marvels of human experience, especially in prison, that a man can feel that much anger inside and appear calm on the outside. It takes practice, but you would be surprised how much control can be exercised when the alternative is lethal.

I spent hours circling the exercise yard pondering, searching. My new faith felt like an empty shell. God appeared indifferent, distant, way beyond the high fences topped with razor wire. I wasn't angry at him. I was just angry. Angry at this miserable life I was living. Angry at the years of time that lay ahead. Angry at some of the people I was forced to live with. Angry others had such complete power over my freedom. Angry my dad was gone, just as we were beginning to put the pieces of a broken relationship back together.

Ours had been a rough road. I had brought great pain into his life. Now, any chance of atoning for that was gone.

A couple of days after receiving the news, as I drifted around the exercise yard, one of the guys from my range came up alongside me.

"Hank. Here's something to help you out." He handed over a couple of joints. "It's good stuff. If you need more just let me know."

It was a gesture of kindness layered in darkness for someone like me. It was not the first time I had been offered drugs since arriving in prison. I had always refused, well aware of what would happen when I started using.

Unlike others, who could get high once in a while and walk away, I could never get enough. There was a constant need for more.

I rolled the joints over in my hand. *Why did I take them? I have God in my life. He's supposed to be sufficient for all my needs. Surely, I don't need to get high again. I left all that behind. I don't need this garbage to deal with life.*

As the arguments bounced around in my head, my hand raised one of the joints to my mouth. The other hand found the lighter in my jacket. I sucked the smoke in with a mix of dread and relief.

By the time the joint was finished, the world was a much calmer place. Rage gave way to peace. Razor wire and fence faded into oblivion. The snake pit of emotions drifted away as aimlessly as the clouds in the sky that were captivating me.

What a great place to be! I was high and I didn't care. The only two thoughts floating through my mind were: *I wish this wouldn't end. It would sure be nice to get something with more kick to it.*

Drifting back to my cell, I stashed the other joint and crashed.

My *Dark Night of the Soul* had begun, and I had no idea someone had crafted such a dismal term for it.

The Hound of Heaven

Mine was a gradual, methodical drift away from God.

The usual cycle sprang up. Get high. Feel bad. Do it again. What did it matter?

I was stuck here, going nowhere. Getting high just made it more bearable. Over time it dulled any desire for prayer, reflection, or divine connection. I continued to go to Chapel sporadically. It became more of a social connection than a spiritual one. High or not, I would show up at Chapel, although being there, spaced out, was not very comfortable.

Then my reason for going to Chapel shifted entirely. I met someone, and a relationship started to blossom. She was a university student who attended one of our regular Chapel groups.

It wasn't long before she had to give up her attendance in the group. We began seeing each other in the Visiting Area of the institution.

It was a rocky relationship from the start. I was an immature twenty-two-year-old who didn't have a clue about what a loving relationship looked like. Relationships were a maze of confusion for me. More often than not, in my short stint of freedom on the street, drugs trumped relationships.

Prison relationships are often doomed from the start. Very few survive. How do you make something so strange work? She wasn't from my world, and I wasn't from hers. Despite the warnings, the well-meaning advice, the nagging persistent doubts, I jumped in with everything I had, completely lost in love.

I saw nothing else in my future outside of her. I even managed to get an engagement ring. I showed up at a visit with it and asked her to marry me.

She was shocked. When she took the ring and didn't give

me a direct answer, I knew something was up. But, by that point, it didn't matter. The drift was complete. I was boxed in. My future world was all about her and I could see no other.

Interesting how we can so easily delude ourselves into thinking everything is alright, only to have the truth burst into our lives at the most unwanted of times.

I am not sure when it started. Maybe it was always there, but at some point, the still presence of the Holy Spirit began to grow annoyingly loud in my conscience. I suspect it took root the day Gerry Fuller, the student prison chaplain, showed up on our range.

I was very high that weekend. I don't know what they had laced the joints with, but it was good. It probably didn't help that I had popped a few pills also.

Suddenly I heard a voice—a familiar one—asking if I was around.

No, it can't be him! I thought.

But when I threw my cell door open, there he was. I was shocked, then angry, an unusual reaction for me when I was that high.

Gerry stood there, grinning away. "Hi, Hank, how are you doing?"

Now, there are some taboos in prison. Gerry broke one of them when he decided to take a walk down to the unit on a Saturday evening.

There he stood, every con on the range glaring at the heat score[3] that had just arrived at my cell.

I was dumbfounded. I couldn't believe he would pull a stunt like this. You don't step onto a prison range out of the blue to

---

[3] A "heat score" is someone who draws unwanted attention to a situation. In this situation, Gerry's presence on the range would have made staff more attentive to the range.

"visit" someone, especially in off hours. Who knows what you are going to see or what the guys might be up to?

I pulled him into my cell. "What the hell are you doing here?"

Smiling away, he said, "Oh, just wanted to see how you were doing."

"Well, Gerry. This is not a good time."

"Oh. Okay. Could we have a word of prayer?"

"No!"

By that point, he was picking up on the fact that I really didn't want him around.

As he got up to leave, it was apparent that he was hurt by the cold shoulder. "Okay. I'll see you in Chapel, Hank."

I liked Gerry, but sometimes he was over the top. So much for a nice high.

I felt like a hypocrite. He had come to see me with good intentions—naive ones, but good ones—and, instead of getting a warm reception, he got a stoned, angry con. He didn't deserve that. He meant well.

Had I known then what his future held, I would have let him pray.

On the outside I looked fine, just like any other guy doing time. But on the inside, a war was erupting. It had started out as small skirmishes in my conscience, small pangs of guilt that were soon set adrift with a joint, some good hash, THC, Angel Dust, pills, whatever was available.

Gabor Maté in his book, *In the Realm of Hungry Ghosts*, heads one of the chapters with a quote that neatly captures my state of mind at the time: "A Void I'll Do Anything to Avoid." My relationship with the love of my life, the one my future hopes hung on, was getting rockier by the month. Like a sailor tossed overboard in a storm, I was grasping for some kind of floating debris to hang on to—a fleeting phone call, or a letter that spoke nothing about what was really going on. Desperately, I tried to delude myself into believing all was well.

Wars inevitably reach a tipping point—a quick, decisive action, or a slow chiselling at the others' battered defences. The latter was my demise. The opening lines of Francis Thompson's poem *The Hound of Heaven* fit all too well:

> I fled Him, down the nights and down the days;
> I fled Him, down the arches of the years;
> I fled Him, down the labyrinthine ways
>   Of my own mind; and in the mist of tears
> I hid from Him, and under running laughter.
>   Up vistaed hopes, I sped;
>   And shot, precipitated,
> Adown Titanic glooms of chasmed fears,
>   From those strong Feet that followed, followed after.
>   But with unhurrying chase,
>   And unperturbed pace,
>   Deliberate speed, majestic instancy,
>   They beat—and a Voice beat
>   More instant than the Feet—
> "All things betray thee, who betrayest Me."[4]

It was a slow, painful, overwhelming realization that forced me back to my knees. My crafted veil of illusion was slowly being pulled aside. I saw myself travelling down the same dark path that had brought me to prison.

I wept, not with physical tears, but far deeper. I wept in my soul, in a place no one sees but God. My plea for forgiveness contained no flowery words. Instead, I lifted up the plea of a

---

[4] Francis Thompson's poem can be found in full at The Project Gutenberg as listed in the bibliography.

desperate man. "Please, God, help me live clean, one day at a time."

The road grew darker, one hand desperately hanging on to God and trying to clean up my life, the other firmly holding on to a relationship that had no hope.

Torn between two worlds, I wrestled to stay in control. Surely, God was not going to ask me to give up this relationship too. She was the love of my life. It would all work out. Little did I know the prophetic power of Francis Thompson's poetic words—"All things betray thee, who betrayest Me."

I should have known. The words were written by an opium addict.

The Abyss

The truth rarely comes in one sharp flash. It often surfaces by imposing itself in small moments of insight that build on one another.

A rumour began to surface. The love of my life was seeing someone else. I am not sure where I first heard it. I dismissed it. Then it surfaced again. Still I refused to pay attention. It wasn't until a close friend came over to talk that the ugly truth roared from behind closed doors.

He arrived with a joint in hand. "Here, you are going to need this."

I refused. "What's up?" I asked.

This was not the kind of conversation friends like to have with each other, especially in prison, but he told me, in unadulterated detail. She was seeing someone else, had been for months. That was tough enough. But what I learned next tore me apart. The person she was seeing was the brother of a man who worked in the prison.

The reality of the situation didn't take long to sink in. While I dreamed of life with no one else but her, some staff—I never knew how many—were aware that she was seeing someone else.

An angry phone call confirmed the truth. The term "played for a fool" did not come close to describing the scenario unfolding in my head. I felt like a pawn in a game.

In my mind all I could hear were the voices of staff snickering and joking in their offices, control posts, or having a few beers at the local pub, laughing at the dumb lifer. And if they knew, so did some of the guys around me.

In the days to come, as I walked through the prison, I found myself wondering, *How many know?*

This was uncharted territory. My mind began to go places it had not been for some time—dangerous, volatile places. This was a new kind of pain. External pain I understood. A punch, a hit, a kick, these I could connect to some outside action. But when the same kind of pain erupts from within, there is no escape, especially in prison. Everywhere you go, circling the yard surrounded by fences, razor wire, and towers, all mocking your miserable life, in your cell, at work, on the range—it was there, screaming at you, clawing away at your sanity with no way to shut it off, an all-consuming pain so intense it cripples your capacity to think, to react normally to the outside world.

To those around, it was evident I was not doing well. I was spaced out, withdrawn, even refusing to get high. Somehow, I knew. I had moved past the point where any "self-medication" would touch this pain. I wondered, *Am I going insane? Is this what it feels like to lose it?*

A fog set in, a blurring between reality and unreality. I was beginning to slip. All the wild drug trips I had been on, the mind-altering hallucinogens which had sailed me into bizarre other worlds—they were nothing like this.

I am not sure staff were concerned about my mental health. I suspect they were a great deal more worried about what would erupt from a messed-up kid doing life for murder.

I was soon called to the Unit Office to talk with my assigned Living Unit Officer.[5] After numerous questions about how I was doing, which I no doubt answered incoherently, he was called out of the room. Left alone in the office, a bewildering array of bizarre thoughts rushed through my mind.

I suddenly found myself standing over an open cauldron, my feet right on the edge of it. I looked down into the deep gaping hole to see a dark, swirling, slowly churning mass. In an instant, I knew what I was looking at. An escape! All I needed to do was lean forward, fall into the abyss, and let go of my sanity.

It was that simple. No more pain. As I stared into the cauldron of confusion and oblivion there was no strength left.

I was empty. It wasn't just losing what I thought was the love of my life. It was everything.

What kind of life was this? I was in control of nothing, a puppet on the end of a string manipulated by others.

Leaning forward, I could feel the strength of the cauldron's pull. Then, just as I was about to lose my balance, a firm hand clasped my shoulder. I hung there for a moment, suspended over my plunge out of pain.

I didn't have to turn and look. The moment the hand touched me, I knew who it was. He didn't say anything. The firm

---

[5] In the federal prison system inmates are assigned a Correctional Officer as part of their Case Management Team. Today they are known as CX2's. During my time in prison, and in the specific structure of the institution, the individual was a called a Living Unit Officer.

grip communicated everything it needed to as He gently pulled me back.

Emotions began to overwhelm me. The next thing I knew, I was out of the office, quickly walking back to my cell.

I sat on the bunk, drained of strength, in awe of a God who cared that much. I looked over to the small desk in my cell. Above it, stuck to the wall, was a picture I had received a year earlier from one of the chaplains.

At the end of a difficult conversation, he had given it to me. It was a small pocket-size picture, a print of a painting by Warner Sallman titled, *Christ, Our Pilot*. It showed a young man with his hands on a ship's wheel, navigating through rough seas. On his left shoulder rests the hand of Jesus Christ, who is standing behind him. The Lord's other hand is pointing the way forward.

I had no idea what the way forward was. But I did know the hand that rested on my shoulder, and that was enough.

Integration

As I started to emotionally and mentally claw my way back toward stable ground, the only certainty in my life was that Jesus Christ was in my corner. Everything else was on shaky ground.

Even that certainty was tested on occasion, whenever I would dwell on the twisting, painful reality of losing a dream and putting life back together.

In one of those moments, when waves of loss and darkness crashed over me, threatening to crush my hold on sanity, I had another encounter with the living Christ which is too personal to share. Suffice it to say, it was a profound assurance that the words of the prophet Isaiah were as relevant in my situation as when they were first written:

He was despised and rejected by mankind,
a man of suffering, and familiar with pain.
Like one from whom people hide their faces
he was despised, and we held him in low esteem.

(Isaiah 53:3)

This was a whole new side of faith I had never contemplated before. The idea that God not only understood my suffering, but had experienced his own loss, pain, and anguish, far beyond what I could imagine. He knew betrayal. He knew loss. He knew loneliness in a way that was deeply moving. It was a revelation I firmly clung to, because I was terribly alone.

I was faced with an isolation that was difficult to break out of. Who could I talk to about what was happening to me?

I was stuck in what could be termed a lifer's dilemma. I was serving time for the most violent of offences. Talking to a psychologist—even requesting to do so—would be opening a Pandora's box. This was the 1980s. Religion and psychology didn't mix well. Knowing that if I recounted my journey, I'd risk it being recorded on a file for others to poke and prod was enough to convince me I would have to keep all of this close to my chest. The last thing I needed was another label to battle.

One would assume the chaplains were safe to talk with, but assumptions of trust in prison can net you a great deal of trouble. I had already seen a hint of this. When I arrived at Springhill Institution from the Max, I shared my dramatic conversion with a few people. The reception ranged from "Interesting" to "Is this guy in his right mind?"

I was taking no more chances. Quietly, I continued to wrestle through the confusion on my own. The problem was, I didn't have a very big toolbox to work with. As far as I was concerned, the evangelical theology I had so doggedly clung to since my conversion had failed me. My journey of faith was not fitting into any kind of evangelical storyline.

There was a fractured sanity to my existence. In the center was an unshakable knowledge that God's hand was at work. But beyond that, everything was in flux: my understanding of God, my relationship with Him, the purpose of my life, what the future held, why I was even alive and sane.

Eventually I decided to take a chance. With great trepidation, I managed to corner someone whom I had been watching and listening to for some time.

I didn't know it then, but Charlie Taylor was one of the grandfathers of Clinical Pastoral Training in Canada. He specialized in prison ministry. For years, prior to my arrival at Springhill, Charlie and his wife Charlotte had been travelling up to Springhill regularly to conduct and lead the Kairos Marathon Encounter groups in the Chapel.[6] Their non-judgemental attitude, filled with a grace and hopefulness toward those who were so alienated from society, spoke volumes about the true nature of their faith.

In a quiet conversation at the back of the Chapel, I shared a small part of my journey with Charlie, just enough to test the water. The impact of that conversation would resonate throughout my entire life and ministry.

Charlie listened carefully and then began to talk about the early Christian mystics, the Desert Fathers, and the rich tradition of mysticism that was woven into the history of the church. The more he talked, the more I was drawn in.

That conversation was the catalyst, the beginning point of a

---

[6] Dr. Charles Taylor was Professor of Clinical Pastoral Education at Acadia Divinity College. He was the founder of the Kairos Marathon Encounter Groups, which he started in 1969. The following is a link to information on his life: http://acadiadiv.ca/taylor/about/

transforming journey of integration. As I read more about Christian mysticism and those who had travelled its varied roads, my faith was strengthened. I had a theological structure to understand my experience in. My faith was not being torn apart. It was being rebuilt in ways that I could never have imagined.

A number of years after my release, I decided to have a look at my prison records via a Freedom of Information Request. Buried on one page of my medical file is this cryptic note dated January 7, 1981, just a few days after my encounter with the abyss: "Seen last charting. 'Personal problems.' Says he feels ok now. Doesn't want any further medication as drug problem in the past and off everything for 4 months." I never took drugs again.

Charlie, Charlotte, and I became very close. We shared numerous moving conversations about this mysterious journey God was crafting in each of our lives. After my release, I made many trips to Wolfville, Nova Scotia, to visit with them. It was a restoring refuge. Charlotte's wonderful hospitality and the grace-filled conversations that would transpire after a lunch or dinner with both of them are still with me today.

In 2004, Charlie was inducted into the Order of Canada for his work with those in prison. I was asked to be one of the speakers at the induction. Unfortunately, distance and finances prevented me from attending. Instead, I wrote a poem which I asked a friend to read. It was dedicated to both Charlie and Charlotte.

The Vision

Oh how they've asked from time to time,
as I have worked in this calling that is mine.
Why are you here of all places to be,
in a prison where time wastes men's souls away?

What makes a man who has served his time,
nine long years with life parole,
come back to this hell to work and care.
Surely there's something not right with you.

Perhaps you're just a little bit insane.
Or maybe the guilt was too much to bear,
and now you're still trying to atone for your sins.
Surely a man who walks back in isn't quite right.

I smile, as they ponder the mystery of my life,
as they wonder and probe what I'm all about.
Little do they know, that I came back in,
because of a vision that caressed my soul.

It wasn't one so dramatic as Paul's
on his way to destroy God's holy work.
Mine was a vision that took some time,
filled with moments of penetrating light.

I first saw them in an unlikely place,
a house of worship within the walls.
I hardly noticed when I first met them,
they weren't from my world, or so I thought.

The weeks went by and the months moved on.
Time and again they kept coming back, I started to ask,
why are you here of all places to be,
in a prison where time wastes men's souls away?

I didn't ask them with words and talk.
Years of prison had taught me well,
that words mean nothing.
Watch their actions, that's what counts.

I watched them closely, listening as they spoke,
and slowly an answer began to emerge.
Not one that was spoken by them alone,
but one that echoed through the hallways of time.

It was an answer I found so hard to believe,
an answer so simple yet hard to conceive,
an answer with power beyond all I had known
…God is Love.

How could it be that these simple words,
would compel two people to give of their lives,
for the rebels and outcasts,
the hopeless and lost.

I had to find out what made them come.
Maybe they weren't quite right, you know.
I had to find out if this God they knew,
was the very same God I was coming to know.

The weeks went by and the months moved on.
Our friendship grew, as we journeyed on,
and a heart like a stone,
was softened and warmed in the light of their love.

It was a difficult day when the first calling came.
It was hard to believe that God wanted me,
to shepherd and care for His very own.
Surely, they didn't want someone like me.

I wondered and pondered and thought God was wrong,
till Charlie one day unveiled God's touch,
    in the heart of my life.
With a word from the Spirit, he reminded me
that the Master's hand always guides in love.

The journey continued through school and church,
where the title Reverend was placed by my name.
Then in the midst of my journey in life, a call came again,
to a place I dared not face.

I walked back into the darkness and rage.
I hated prison, with its fences and walls,
with its iron and concrete so hard and cold,
with its empty lives and broken dreams.

It was the journey to Seg that shook my core.
Each cell filled with more bitterness and rage.
From time to time as I gazed on a face,
a reflection from the past charged back through my soul.

I stood at his door as he glared at me.
He turned his back and declared with disgust,
this is who I adore and serve.
The words "Child of Satan" tattooed cross his back.

"So, what the hell are you doing here?"
Contempt and hate oozed from his words.
I pondered his question and began to smile,
I knew the answer deep within.

In words his soul was meant to hear,
in a language this dark place understood.
With a heart set free in that same dark pit
I revealed to him that…God is Love.

And so I discovered on a prison range,
that a vision had been imparted to me.
A vision of light, a vision of hope
a vision I bore wherever I went.

Some claim great saints exist,
in far-off places and far-off lands.
Perhaps they're right, perhaps they're not,
for I have walked with two so close to you.

Today as you award this honour of light,
remember that among you sit,
two of God's Holy Saints.
Who if asked will tell you…God is Love.

Dr. Charles Taylor was inducted into the Order of Canada
On May 21, 2004. On June 10, 2004, at the age of 86, he went

to be with the Lord. On Wednesday, September 9, 2009, Charlotte joined him.[7]

---

[7] In November of 2001, the Correctional Service of Canada named their annual volunteer award after Charlie and Charlotte, https://www.csc-scc.gc.ca/volunteers/003008-1000-eng.shtml

3. A Theological Model
of Change

*You do not delight in sacrifice, or I would bring it;
you do not take pleasure in burnt offerings.
The sacrifices of God are a broken spirit;
a broken and contrite heart,
O God, you will not despise.
(Psalm 51:16-17)*

Christian conversion in prison is complex, confusing, and in some cases completely transforming. It is fraught with twists and turns, ups and downs, humiliating honesty, and its polar opposite—manipulative deception. It is not, as some suppose, a black-and-white, radically changing decision. Instead, it is filled with grey zones that utterly perplex those who believe they have their Christian theology all figured out.

Exploring this experience pushes the boundaries for those who like to adhere to what can be termed a cookie cutter approach to change—a "magic theology" view that one size fits all.

Magic theology undermines a central dynamic of the Christian faith: a growing relationship with Jesus Christ. It comes from a position of trying to control, manipulate, use—all of which hampers growth because real growth in faith comes through surrender.

The apostle Peter's encounter with Simon the Sorcerer (Acts 8:9-24) is a good example of how God views magic theology.

Seeing the great miracles that Philip was performing and how people received the Holy Spirit when the apostles laid hands on them, Simon the Sorcerer wanted the same power. He offered money to the apostles for the power to do the same. Peter firmly rebuked Simon: "May your money perish with you, because you thought you could buy the gift of God with money! You have no part or share in this ministry, because your heart is not right before God." (Acts 8:20-21)

Simon made the mistake of believing that the power of the Holy Spirit was something he could possess and control for his own purposes. Being a former sorcerer, Simon wanted to impress people with this new power, but for all the wrong reasons. The apostles understood that these manifestations of God's great power were not for or about them personally. These works were God manifesting himself so others might be drawn to Him. Simon simply wanted to do what he had always done—control and impress people.

Disconnect

It was 1980, and I had four years in on my sentence. The prison Chapel at Springhill Medium Security Institution had become a central part of my life. A guest speaker was coming in who had served years in prison, come to faith in Christ, and was now on a speaking circuit at prisons throughout the country.

The Chapel was filled with a mixed bag of individuals that evening. Some were regular Chapel attenders. Others came to grab a coffee. A few were there to check out this curiosity. I sat at the back, along with a couple other Chapel regulars.

He turned out to be a dynamic speaker. It was evident his

life had undergone a radical change. I was impressed. Then, when the altar call[8] came, things started to look different.

Two things surprised me as people went forward. First, there were the numbers. Usually, only a few men would go forward to an altar call. This time twenty out of a group of sixty men went up.

More disturbing, though, was the fact that a number of the men who went forward had done so before when previous speakers had come in and given their altar call.

I was having a hard time fitting their actions into my novice understanding of the Christian faith. One of the realities of being in prison for a few years is that you get to know something about most of the people around you. You learn who is dealing drugs, loan sharking, muscling, dangerous, or likes using younger inmates for sex. You know who can be trusted, to some degree, and those who have no idea what the word trust means. You know who is living out their faith and who is playing the game. You know those who are trying to change and those who are simply painting a nice picture, looking for an easy get out of jail card.

It was coffee time. As I stood in the corner mulling over the events of the evening, the speaker came over with a young inmate in tow.

"Hank, I understand you are one of the really solid Chapel guys here. I was wondering if you could do something for me? James just made a commitment of faith and I was wondering if you could take him under your wing and help him out."

This was a surprise, and not a pleasant one. I knew some

---

[8] An altar call is a tradition in some Christian faith traditions whereby individuals are invited to publicly declare a new commitment to Jesus Christ by coming forward to the front of the church building. The name is derived from the altar being located at the front of the church.

things about James. He was a messed up young man, doing a
short sentence, and was running with a dangerous crew. To add
another layer of trouble, there were rumours he was doing sexual
favours.

I pondered the speaker's request. I didn't want to get caught
up in this young man's world. As I stood looking at him, I
wondered how real his "conversion" was. On the other hand, if it
was real, I had a responsibility to try and help him out.

Reluctantly, I said, "Okay."

With that, the speaker was gone to see someone else. James
and I were left looking at each other. He was uncomfortable. I
was taken aback that the speaker, a man who had served time
himself, would throw me into a situation like this.

"James," I said, "I am going to leave this in your ballpark. I
am around if you need to talk."

He nodded and joined his friends on the other side of the
room. Over the next few weeks, I tried to connect with James as
we passed each other in the yard or breezeway. I had little success.
He showed up one Sunday for Chapel, stayed a few minutes, then
left.

Eventually, he was released. I never heard how he made out.

So, a speaker comes in to hold an evangelistic crusade—a
man who served time himself, someone who should know the lay
of the land. Twenty men went forward and made commitments
of faith. Did our Chapel numbers go up? Not one bit. Were
numerous lives transformed? Well, having watched this same
scenario play out a few times, I decided to keep a watchful eye on
a number of the men who went forward. The vast majority went
right back to doing the very things they had been doing before.
If any lives had been dramatically changed that evening, I saw no
evidence of it.

This experience would have been relegated to the dust bin
of long forgotten memories except for one thing. Weeks later, I

heard the evangelist who had come into Springhill was speaking at numerous venues in the community. He was telling everyone about all the men who had made commitments of faith. He was letting the world know about the hundreds of men whose lives had been changed through his work in prisons.

Disbelief was my first reaction. The second was disappointment. The third, frustration that someone who had served time would have such a simplistic perspective on conversion. Surely, he should know better. Evidently, he didn't, or he chose not to acknowledge the truth of the situation.

Though this occurred over forty years ago, it remains lodged in my memory because it underlines a difficult issue surrounding conversion on the inside: the disconnect that often exists with Christians on the "outside" regarding the reality of conversion inside a prison.

Over the years, I have watched the difficulties well-meaning Christians get into when this disconnect plays itself out. It can get ugly.

> The volunteer who spent weeks, months, maybe years investing time and energy into an inmate, only to watch the former inmate's life spiral out of control when they get out of prison. He claimed to be a new man, yet the test of street life quickly tore the facade away and the old man appeared again.

> The lady who came in as a volunteer and thought she had found true love behind the walls with a man who claimed to be transformed. After his release, she discovered his truth was a finely-crafted illusion. The real truth: she was not the

first one he had walked down the garden path of his deception.

The inmate released from prison and recommended to a local community outreach program, who turned out to be anything but rehabilitated. At first all seemed to go well. He slowly gained the trust of an outreach worker who poured energy and time into his life only to have this "changed man" assault and rob him weeks later.

There are other stories I could share, in painful detail. They are the dark side of the conversion story.

Yet, there is another side. In parallel with these dark stories of dashed hopes, deception, and violence are a few others where lives have been completely transformed. They are miracles. There is no other word that captures the changes I have witnessed in men's lives, including my own. So, how is anyone supposed to make sense of all this?

The most important place to start is with an understanding that conversion looks very different inside a prison compared to outside of it. There are dynamics at work in an institution which impact the way conversion is perceived and lived out. And none has a greater impact then the quick fix myth.

The Quick Fix Myth

I sat in my office at Open Circle staring out the window, frustration and fatigue mixing together as I tried to process the suicide that had happened. There had been so many over the years—friends, acquaintances, enemies. I never got used to it, no matter how often I had to deal with it. I was always left with an empty frustration, a forceful reminder that life can become unbearably hard, to the point where it blinds a person to any other option.

Suicides are a part of prison life. On occasion, they can hit with a force I was unprepared for. This was one of them.

Two weeks earlier, I had visited Terry, letting him know that we had found a volunteer to match him with. He was upbeat and looking forward to someone coming to see him regularly.

He committed suicide the day before we were able to connect him with a volunteer visit.

As is so often the case with suicide, the carefully crafted mask people wear never conveys the true depth of their inner turmoil. During my visits with Terry, two clues emerged that the struggles in his life were taking on darker tones. He uttered two statements, each at a different visit, which I joked had made him the philosopher of Stony Mountain.

One afternoon, we sat talking about his see-saw life of returning to prison repeatedly for behaviours he neither appeared to want to control, or at times, had the capacity to control.

He said, "The end is the beginning and the beginning is the end."

I sat for a moment, surprised by his insight. "Do you really feel that way?"

"Yeah," he replied. "I'm tired of this life. Somehow I need to do something about it."

In retrospect, I now see how that particular comment dovetailed with the one he voiced at the prior visit. As we joked about his new standing as a philosopher, Terry had said, "Why is the easy road always the hard road, and the hard road is always the easy road?"

In that earlier visit, we sat in the visiting area quietly

unpacking Terry's tough reality. His life had consisted of taking the easy road and thumbing his nose at the world. Here he was, again, back in prison.

The easy road had resulted in hard consequences. A long list of strict conditions was in place for his release into the community. They would dramatically impact his freedom on the street.

To move forward, Terry knew the easy road was no longer an option. The hard road was the only way forward, with the hope it would eventually become an easier road. But there was a catch. It was going to be a very long, hard road before it got easier. Ultimately, Terry decided the reward for travelling the long hard road was too far away and not worth pursuing.

Terry's story remains with me, a reminder of the harsh reality that, for those who travel through the criminal justice system, change can be a life and death struggle. There is no shortcut.

Shortcuts are a myth. There are no quick fixes. There are no instant cures. And when it comes to Christian conversion and change, there is no magic.

Those who have spent a great deal of time researching conversion in prison have come to realize they often do not last. Byron Johnson, a leading researcher in the area of Christian religion in prison, discovered this reality in his own dissertation work.

Over a ten-year period, he tracked men released from a prison in Florida who had reported a born-again experience. He discovered there was no difference in recidivism rates compared to released individuals who did not have a conversion.[9] This sobering statistic is helpful to remember when ministering with

---

[9] From page 160 of *More God Less Crime: Why Faith Matters and How it Could Matter More*, by Byron R. Johnson.

individuals in prison. Conversion, in and of itself, provides absolutely no assurance that a person will go on to lead a law-abiding life. In fact, in some cases, I would argue it can be an impediment.

Some readers may see this comment as bordering on heresy. Let me explain.

It is estimated almost seventy percent of inmates entering the Canadian Correctional system have a substance abuse problem.[10] As a former addict, I have lived out one of the hallmarks of addiction. It morphs into the ultimate escape engine for life's immediate problems. When you marry this to some of the conversion theology that finds its way into our prisons, a serious problem surfaces.

One of my favourite verses in Scripture is found in 2 Corinthians 5:17:

"Therefore if anyone is in Christ, he is a new creation, the old has gone, the new has come!"

Taken at face value, this statement seems to imply that if you will just let Jesus Christ into your life, you will become brand new, instantaneously. Men whose world view consists of using quick fixes to deal with life's problems, find elements of the gospel message tremendously appealing. They are told to simply voice the sinner's prayer and it is done. You are now a Christian, and God will begin his great work in your life.

Inevitably, our Lord's parable about the sower and the seeds (Matthew 13:1-23) speaks with prophetic power into prison conversions. Many fall away, and some become bitter and resentful. The promise didn't pan out. The tough temptations returned. The old crowd whispered in their ear, and they could

---

[10] From https://www.csc-scc.gc.ca/research/forum/e133/e133 c-eng.shtml on the Forum on Corrections Research of the Correctional Service of Canada Website.

not stay away. The hard-con image was too useful as an intimidation tactic to let go of.

I have lost count of the number of men who have told me about making a commitment of faith, only to eventually walk away, or worse. They had their commitment torn apart by the conflicts of life—much as I did, walking around a prison yard trying to grapple with the impact of my father's death, facing the hard reality of prison and sliding back into drugs.

For some, this failure is overwhelming. It is painful to sit in an office with a young man back on a parole violation, hearing how he left prison filled with assurance that his newfound faith would see him through the tough times, believing the "old man" was gone and the new had arrived, only to find himself here, sitting in my office, devastated, questioning the very existence of God.

For the more theologically-minded reader, the views presented in this chapter closely mirror a process well known to Christians: sanctification. This is understood to be the continuing work of God in a believer's life, through the indwelling of the Holy Spirit, who is shaping and forming the believer to become holy. In this context, the word holy can be understood as "bearing an actual likeness to God".[11]

But sanctification looks different in prison. It has unique aspects chaplains and volunteers should be aware of.

The Model

For years I searched to find a model that would capture my journey of conversion, change, and ministry, not so much for

---

[11] From page 967 of *Christian Theology*, by Millard Erikson.

myself, but for others. Repeatedly, my attempts to communicate the complex, confusing, complicated, and in some cases transforming nature of conversion and change in prison fell short of the mark. My desire to communicate this process was anchored in the reality that my experience mirrored the pilgrimage of others encountering Christ in prison, a journey that some Christians had difficulty grasping.

A model arrived at my doorstep in a way that can only be termed a classic God maneuver. It wasn't a great theologian who delivered it. Instead, it was a former heroin addict who came to speak at a Chapel service at Atlantic Institution while I was chaplain there.

As he shared his own story of transformation, one filled with twists and turns before staying clean, it was evident he was a man steeped in life on the streets and the hard, destructive road of drug abuse. Part way through his presentation, he began moving over toward the left wall in the Chapel.

As he approached the wall, he looked at us. "Imagine that this wall is darkness, evil." Then he looked at the other wall to the right of us. "Now imagine that the wall over there is light, God's transforming light." He then turned to face the dark wall and pressed his face into it. "This is where I was at one point in my life. This is where some of you are, completely immersed in darkness. You can't see anything in front of you except darkness. Then, a glimmer of light catches your attention, or suddenly, by some miracle the light penetrates through you to reveal a glimmer of hope. You turn your head to look. Captivated, you turn to face the light on the other wall."

As he turned to look toward the wall of light he said, "This is conversion, a turning to face the light."

He had my attention. What he said next revealed that I had found my model.

"After we turn toward the light, we spend the rest of our

lives moving toward the light." He moved a few feet toward the wall of light, then stopped. "Sometimes we stall. Sometimes we take a few steps back. We might even turn to look back at the dark and feel pulled there."

Quickly, it became clear why a former heroin addict working with addicts would find such a model helpful. There is a hard truth about addictions that certain Christians find difficult to accept—that of relapse. Those who work in the field of addictions are well aware relapse is often a part of the path to sobriety.

But for some Christians, relapse flies in the face of conversion. If you are a "new creation", how could you possibly fall back into the same old pattern of behaviour? After all, there are stories of people who have cleaned up their lives through conversion and never drank or used again.

But here is where the standard conversion storyline creates a problem. It is not the normal course of change for addicts. Longitudinal research, which is research that measures people over a period of time, shows that religious involvement alone is rarely enough to bring about a dramatic transformative lasting change with regard to addiction.[12] If this insight is coupled with an earlier figure presented—that seventy percent of individuals entering prison suffer from a substance abuse problem—it becomes apparent why criminal behaviour is also prone to relapse. Yet, even with these insights, we continue to perpetuate the storyline that conversion will solve the problem.

Why? Because it is convenient and sells well. Simplistic answers to complex problems have always been the default

---

[12] From page 264 of *Rethinking Substance Abuse: What Science Shows and What we Should do about it* by Keith Humphreys and Elizabeth Gifford, the chapter titled, "Religion, Spirituality, and Troublesome Use of Substances".

position for those who are afraid to ask hard questions and explore the truth fully. Exploring those hard questions can challenge a person's worldview in uncomfortable ways.

I recall a friend of mine once hearing from a new part time chaplain starting at an institution. The new chaplain had no experience in prison chaplaincy and no training in the area. At the end of the first week, he informed my friend he had "saved" five men that week.

When I hear stories such as this, I am filled with sadness for two reasons.

First, the individual prisoners who found their way to this particular chaplain were met by someone who had no idea what the prison landscape of conversion and change looked like. In the new chaplain's estimation, the best thing he could do was convert as many people as possible. He saw his role solely as that of an evangelist.

Secondly, the individuals coming to see him were probably in far greater need of a shepherd than an evangelist. I can recall how, in my earlier encounters with Christians, more than one well-meaning chaplain or volunteer attempted to convert me after the fact. All they saw was a hardened con who kept his distance. They never bothered to sit, listen, and hear my story. Even if they did, some may well have attempted to get me to say the sinner's prayer again, just to be sure.

Those encounters were disheartening as I attempted to discover my place in the body of Christ.

Starting Point

One of the most powerful truths this model can communicate to those interested in prison ministry is that we do not all have the same starting point in faith. Let's look at two composite individuals, Jeff and Daniel, to understand this better.[13]

Jeff is serving time for manslaughter. Daniel attends church in a small rural congregation.

Jeff

Jeff entered the world with the deck stacked against him. His mother left home at an early age to escape an abusive father. On the streets, alone, she did what she had to do to survive. At the age of seventeen she gave birth to Jeff. Numerous partners, drugs, alcohol, gangs, and trying to survive the myriad forms of abuse weaving their way through this kind of lifestyle left her with little energy to take care of Jeff. As a result, he grew up fending for himself, learning how to survive any way possible.

Along the way, deep painful scars were etched in his life. Abandoned, alone, attempting to make sense of life, Jeff reached out, only to find the enveloping darkness of a sexual predator. It changed him. A hurting street kid searching for hope was twisted into a young man consumed with anger and mistrust.

One night, while closing a drug deal, the other person tried to cheat him. They made the mistake of insulting Jeff with the wrong words. The knife came out and, in a blanket of rage, Jeff ended another man's life. Now he sat in prison facing an eight-year sentence for manslaughter.

Somewhere in the midst of darkness and pain, Jesus Christ broke through and Jeff turned toward the light.

---

[13] I have chosen to use composites in this discussion for illustration purposes. Jeff and Daniel are constructed from general themes taken from numerous conversion stories that have been shared with me.

Daniel

Daniel was always the rebel in the family. Rules were for other people most of the time. Sunday school teachers wrestled with him and public school was not any different.

His ace in the hole was a charming smile and wit. More than once his parents found themselves at the local school hearing the same line: "You know, he is such a wonderful child, but he is always pushing the boundaries."

Boundary pushing may be how he took on the world, but Daniel had a deep love for his parents. Home life was his sanctuary. The family was very involved in their local church and Daniel along with his brothers and sisters would attend all the functions.

Daniel resisted any kind of faith commitment. Instead, he continued to run the gauntlet of risky behaviours looking for that natural high that came with the occasional fight and racing cars.

The only thing that stopped him from jumping into drugs was his mother. They had a special relationship. Disappointing her on that front would have been too much for him to live with.

One night, Daniel was out with friends racing down the backroads around his country home. He lost control of his vehicle, rolling it several times. He was shaken but physically okay. That close brush with death proved to be the catalyst for a serious change in his life.

A few weeks later, he also turned to face the light.

Contrast

Two stories, two different people... From an outside perspective these journeys look very similar. They appear to follow the same path.

Both men found their naive youthful belief in immortality challenged. Both turned to faith in Jesus Christ, and it looked like their lives were being transformed.

Jeff's commitment of faith was evident for all to see as he walked the prison breezeways and ranges. He was a regular Chapel attender who stood out with his strong knowledge of Scripture and willingness to stand up for his faith.

Daniel also grew in faith, becoming a regular participant at his local church. Soon he was contemplating a move into ministry, one encouraged by his family and church community.

Their paths, however, would soon separate. Within weeks of being released on parole Jeff was battling an old enemy, addiction. Soon he was back in, devastated, alone, wrestling to figure out what went wrong. Daniel, on the other hand, eventually went on to Seminary, pursuing a call into ministry.

Two men, two very different paths. Why? Did one simply lack faith, willpower, perseverance? That is often the judgement made in these comparisons. It's a very unfair judgement, which can be challenged by using the model we have just discussed and asking a simple question:

If you imagine the change model, where would you place Jeff and Daniel between the darkness and light at the point of conversion?

If we assume travelling from darkness to the light is a lifetime journey, it would be fair to position Jeff, with his face up against the darkness, and Daniel, about a quarter of the way to the light.

Why this difference? Jeff was beginning his journey of faith from nothing. In fact, an argument could be made he was starting in the negative.

I would add the example of my life to illustrate this point further. I came to faith in Jesus Christ with a long list of problems. I was a very rebellious young man in addition to being a drug addict. From my earliest memories, I was always trying to push the boundaries. I deeply disliked authority in any form. The reasons for this had deep roots in my life. None of this is unusual in a prison population.

Trevor[14]

A short time ago, I was sitting in the visiting area of Stony Mountain Institution with Trevor, one of our participants in the Open Circle visitation program. He was back inside on a parole violation for using drugs, after he didn't show up for a scheduled drug screening test.

I asked him what happened. A long explanation followed, which he knew didn't hold a great deal of merit. More importantly, he knew the ex-con sitting across the table from him also knew it.

Then he offered a sincere sign of respect. "I didn't connect with you on the street because I was up to no good."

I sat there for a moment pondering the comment. "Thanks, Trevor. I really appreciate that. So, why did you start using again and not attempt to work things out?"

There was a long pause. He looked at me, deep frustration rolling across his face. Then he said something I have heard numerous times before, something I personally understood quite well.

"I hate being controlled."

I smiled knowingly. "Well, I don't think that is working out too well for you, is it?"

---

[14] Trevor is not his real name. Throughout the book I have changed certain names to protect the privacy of those who have been part of my journey.

Trevor smirked and we continued our conversation about the frustration of parole.

Challenges

A pattern emerges, if we consider Jeff's, Trevor's, and my own struggles together.

My own journey of rebellion, drug addiction, running from pain, and trying to sort through my confusing adolescent years left me with more than a drug problem. As with other young men on this path, I wrestled with a stunted emotional and social growth.

When my father died and the reality of prison came roaring to the forefront, I had no mature life skills to work with. I had squandered my early years, living in a fantasy world filled with drugs, alienating myself from much of society unless it involved drugs.

Both Trevor and Jeff wrestled with a deep-seated rebellion I understood well.

Daniel's path in life was very different. Although a bit of a rebel, his upbringing was the opposite of ours. He came from a solid family. Life was good. There was a community that supported him, friends he could share good times with, someone in his life who helped steer him away from drug use. He flourished in his local community well before he came to faith in Christ.

It has been estimated that fifty percent of men and women in Canadian prisons have a history of childhood abuse.[15] This

---

[15] From "History of Childhood Abuse in Populations Incarcerated in Canada: A Systematic Review and Meta-Analysis" by Claire Bodkin, Lucie Pivnick, Susan J. Bondy, Carolyn Ziegler, Ruth Elwood Martin, Carey Jernigan, and

comes as no surprise to those working in Corrections. I would suggest the figure may actually be higher.

This is only one of the challenges facing those who enter prisons. A 2015 Correctional Service of Canada study discovered the following: "Over seventy percent of male offenders met criteria for at least one mental disorder."[16] That rate is substantially higher than the general population.

Here is a statistical breakdown of mental disorders behind bars:

- Mood disorders, 16.9 percent
- Primary psychotic, 3.3 percent
- Alcohol/substance use disorders, 49.6 percent
- Anxiety disorders, 29.5 percent
- Eating disorders, 0.8 percent
- Pathological gambling, 5.9 percent
- Borderline personality disorder, 15.9 percent
- Antisocial personality disorder, 44.1 percent.[17]

Sometimes, well-meaning Christians live with the illusion that coming to faith in Christ will somehow cover over, eliminate, or transform this "baggage" in very short order.

Nothing could be further from the truth in a prison context. The walk toward the light can be painfully slow, with numerous disheartening setbacks, as men face the problems that have destroyed so much of their lives and the lives of others.

Fiona Kouyoumdjian, as found in *American Journal of Public Health*.

[16] From *National Prevalence of Mental Disorders Among Incoming Federally Sentenced Men* by J.N. Beaudette, J. Power, and L. Stewart.

[17] Ibid.

A Lonely Walk of Faith

Let's add another layer of contrast.

At Stony Mountain I oversaw a number of different volunteer groups that came into the Chapel. One group was from Altona. They were a committed group who came out to the Chapel every second month to lead a worship service.

One evening, I was invited to join them for pizza in a local restaurant in Winnipeg. It was the start of a tradition. The round trip from Altona to Stony Mountain was three hours. They'd leave Altona at 4:30 and be at the institution by 6:30. They'd come in, do the service, and on the way back, before continuing on to Altona, would stop in Winnipeg for pizza, around 9:30.

My wife Linda and I would often join them. What made these gatherings so memorable was the fellowship that took place. There was plenty of laughter, sharing, and of course more laughter. Even though we were often tired, we thoroughly enjoyed the encouragement we provided each other.

On more than one occasion, as I sat in the midst of this wonderful group of Christian men and women, my thoughts would drift back to the institution and to the men we had just fellowshipped with. I was well aware of what they were heading back to. They would not find a warm, laughing fellowship back on the prison range—anything but.

It could be a jarring transition, walking from the worship and warm community of the Chapel back into the hard, rough world of prison where religion was often viewed as a crutch for the weak. Many of the men who left the Chapel after a service returned to a lonely spiritual existence.

In fact, being here with these volunteers, now as chaplain, surrounded by laughter instead of prison bars, often reminded me of one powerful experience from my past.

It was New Year's Eve, a year after I had started cleaning up my life. One of the guys on the range popped his head into my cell. "Hank, a couple of your buddies are looking for you."

I sauntered down to the end of the range and was met by two of my fellow Christian brothers. "How's it going, Hank?"

"Not too bad."

"Listen, we have some really good stuff. Why don't you come join us before lockup?"

I was stunned. I couldn't believe what I was hearing. These were two guys who knew me. They were well aware of the battle I had pushed through. Yet here they were, offering to get me high. For a good ten minutes they persisted.

"Guys. I don't want to use. I am done. I can't use."

"Come on. You'll be fine. One time isn't going to kill you."

On and on it went, until finally I had enough. I got up and walked away.

Loneliness takes many forms. That night nearly equalled those first few weeks in prison when I learned quickly that you are utterly alone. No matter what comes at you—despair, threats, violence, depression, fear—you either deal with it or die. I sat on my bunk, crying out to God. It was a long night.

By morning, God had forged a whole new depth to my faith. I wasn't going back to that swirling vortex. I made a vow to myself. No matter how lonely the road became, or how isolated I felt, no one, absolutely no one, was ever going to draw me down a road that would aid in my destruction.

I counted myself fortunate, to have had God's guidance to help me deal with the immense loneliness. Yet, even so, surrounded by laughter with the Altona volunteers, I could never erase from my mind the struggles faced by those on the range while we enjoyed our pizza, and how many had it worse than me.

We don't all start in the same place when we come to faith in Christ. Some come with profound deficits—personal, social, psychological. To assume we all have the same starting point is wishful thinking.

A Dog in a Cage

I have worked with many groups of volunteers in my time as a prison chaplain. One group stands out, but for a different reason than my group from Altona.

This was a faithful group of volunteers from a rural community, who attended prison Chapel services every month. We had gathered together a few minutes before the men were to come down for a service. There was the usual conversation. Then, one of the volunteers voiced a view on prisons that hit a sensitive nerve.

"You know, the problem with our prisons in Canada is that they are just not tough enough. We need to make these places really hard to live in. They are not tough enough. That is why people keep coming back."

I quickly shot back, "So, tell me, what happens when you put a dog in a cage and then beat it with a stick every day?"

The group was shocked at my abrupt response. They were all from farming backgrounds and knew the answer to my question. None of them voiced it.

I continued. "You get one of two things. A dog who runs from human contact, or a dog who, given the chance, will attack you. Do you think it is any different for human beings?"

No one responded. They heard the tone of frustration in my voice.

What they did not know was that earlier that week, I had spent an hour with a young man who was being forced to pay rent on his range by one of the gangs. His first refusal was met with a solid beating. They also didn't see the face of another young man who stopped by the Chapel in profound distress as he wrestled with losing his grandmother while stuck in prison. She was the only stable person in a life marred by abuse and abandonment. Added to these encounters, the volunteers did not know about the suicide that had occurred two weeks earlier. Another young man, so harassed and bullied on his range that he couldn't face it anymore, decided a slow choking death at the end of a homemade rope was the better option.

For the volunteer who initially voiced the comment, corporal punishment was probably a part of his early life. Maybe he even practised it with his children. He assumed more punishment would see lives changed.

This was a man who came faithfully each month to prison to bring the message of God's grace to men in prison. What he missed entirely was where some of the men in prison were starting from.

If physical violence and deprivation were part of a person's life before prison and may have contributed to their being in prison, why would you believe it had the power to change them in prison?

Failure

After my release from prison, it was a surprise to me how quickly the Christian community on the street could judge the failures among themselves and in the world. Are not grace and failure opposite sides of the same coin? They are interlinked: grace is meaningless without failure, and failure is hopeless without grace.

It came as a further surprise to spend years studying in seminary and never find what I would refer to as a practical theology of failure. In retrospect, this should not have been a surprise. After all, Christianity is supposed to be about success, not failure—lives being transformed and changed; new beginnings, new lives.

Christians love to put the dramatic stories on display. The only problem is the dramatic is not the norm.

I have shared the first part of my Christian journey numerous times and often receive positive responses. However, my second fall into drugs and subsequent brush with insanity present challenges for a few. How can someone have such a dramatic conversion and fail? Were they even converted the first time around?

It is into this confusing and sometimes misunderstood aspect of the Christian journey that our model shines its brightest. Understanding conversion as one point on a long journey toward the light provides room for what many will encounter in life: failure.

The stark truth of failure is nowhere more apparent than in prison. Here, failure has brought men and women to the lowest rung of human existence. It is a place where their sins are on full display for others to judge, mock, and hate. This is especially true in our digital age, where anyone in the community can unearth an inmate's dark deeds via a few keystrokes.

Scripture has its fair share of failures. There are any number to choose from. Before we explore one story though, I need to point out that a person's context—their lived experience—can play a role in how the Word is understood and interpreted. This is particularly true with regard to the failures found in Scripture.

The story of King David's desire for Bathsheba, the resulting pregnancy, attempted cover-up, and murder of her husband Uriah is one such story (2 Samuel 11). It is often told to convey God's great forgiveness and has brought comfort to many who are burdened with ugly sins. Most readers, however, who hear or read the story have little personal context onto which to anchor the more disturbing aspects of the story.

How different it reads in another place such as prison.

When you have sat and conversed with a man who meticulously planned the murder of a business partner so he could gain from it, or listened to another who planned the murder of his long-time girlfriend so he could take up with a new lover, you catch a glimpse of the depth of David's sinfulness.

Just like David's, these two murders were methodically planned. They were not heat of the moment aberrations committed in a flash of temporary insanity. They occurred over an extended period of time, during which the value of a human life was carefully weighed against the desires of a human heart on a scale controlled by self-deception. Afterward, the murderers went on to live life as if nothing had happened. Neither the business partner nor the man seeking a new partner wanted to face their crime.

David did not want to face his sin either. His descent into darkness took the most human of paths. He repeatedly tried to hide his indiscretions by attempting to manipulate the situation. He called Uriah back from the battle front in an attempt to get him to sleep with his wife. When that didn't work, he tried to get him drunk. Each failure revealed Uriah the Hittite's integrity, while unmasking for the reader the deception of God's appointed King over Israel. David finally took the final lethal step of having Uriah murdered by sending him back to the battle front and secretly ordering he be left exposed to the fiercest fighting.

Numerous times, in conversations with those in prison for violent offences, I have heard the same excuse David would have crafted in his heart: "I didn't have a choice."

But of course, there was a choice. From our observation post as a reader, we can see that. However, for David, as well as some of the men who fill our prisons, there was no other choice. The scale, controlled by self-deception, tipped firmly on the side of personal desires, providing a powerful blocking agent to their conscience.

An unfortunate aspect of communicating the story of David within the Christian community is that we forget, or simply choose to ignore, the broader frame of the story. David's failure, taken as a singular event, provides a great image of God's forgiveness. There is, however, far more here than just a simple act of forgiveness being communicated. The broader frame of the story is both chilling and deeply humbling.

God and David had a long history. Our first introduction to David is the words of the prophet Samuel rebuking King Saul and informing him that God would replace him with "a man after my own heart" (1 Samuel 13:14). Over the ensuing years, God repeatedly saved David from death, eventually making him King over Israel. Even after witnessing God's great hand of protection and providence over him, David still chose to descend into a rebellious disobedience that saw him orchestrate the murder of one of his most trusted generals and widow the woman he wanted for his own pleasure. Experiencing this type of scenario up close gives new insight into the ugliness of David's sin, and how utterly offensive it was to God.

The most powerful exclamation mark to David's story, the point which highlights how morally low he had sunk, comes when God sends the prophet Nathan to confront him. David had no intention of confessing his sin. The King of Israel had to be challenged, forced to face the overwhelming evidence that he had committed a horrible act before God.

This should sound familiar. Rarely does someone walk into a police station and confess their crimes. The vast majority need to be confronted by an arrest, interrogation, a trial, or spending time in prison before they finally admit to their crime.

Despite all this, his methodical planning, his moral

bankruptcy, his scoffing at God's great blessings—God forgave David. This was a man who believed he knew better and at numerous turns in the story chose to be disobedient. This is a man who only humbled himself when God sent the prophet Nathan to tear away his arrogant facade and dismantle his self-deception.

I have used the term "chilling" to define the larger frame of this story. My reason for doing so is because of a disturbing element in this story: even great people of faith, individuals who have walked with God for years, can descend into an arrogant dismissal of their need to submit to the authority of Almighty God. In the process they leave a wake of devastation, broken lives, ruptured relationships, and shattered victims trying to reconstruct their lives.

Even in the midst of this, God does not give up on the perpetrator. And most amazing of all, He is willing to forgive those who ask.

It would be easy to leave the discussion at this point, but that would not reflect the truth of Scripture, or present an honest picture of failure. There is one last observation to make.

Even though God forgave David, there was a price attached to his disobedience and failure. There always is. God longs to forgive. However, as the story of David makes clear, God does not shelter the sinner from the consequences and cost of their actions. Our prisons are full of men who live with that reality.

Failure defines our limits. Failure challenges our arrogance. Failure leaves us with consequences to work through and live with. It is a part of growing. It shapes our personality.

Failure is a tool in God's hands, used to mould us for His service. And, it can be the turning point, the fork in the road where God has the opportunity to lead us down a path we never knew existed.

4. The Hidden Journey

Therefore, since we are surrounded by
so great a cloud of witnesses,
let us throw off everything that hinders
and the sin that so easily entangles.
And let us run with perseverance
the race marked out for us.
(Hebrews 12:1)

Genesis 4 tells the story of two brothers, Cain and Abel. Abel offers to God an acceptable offering while his brother Cain misses the mark with an offering God does not favour. The incident so angers Cain that he murders his brother. In the first lines of the conversation between God and Cain, we discover an important word:

> Then the Lord said to Cain, "Where is your brother Abel?"
>
> "I don't know," he replied. "Am I my brother's keeper?"
>
> The Lord said, "What have you done? Listen! Your brother's blood cries out to me from the ground."
>
> (Genesis 4:9-10)

It is only one word, but its implications for those of us who have broken, wounded, and destroyed others is profound. As

God confronts Cain, the first thing He challenges him to do is to "Listen!"[18]

Listen, to the cry of your victim rising up to me!

God's requirement of perpetrators has not changed since Genesis. He still insists that we "Listen!"

Listen to the voices of our victims and the victims of others. In the pages to follow, it will become clear why this is so important.

The Answer

The walk was refreshing. With each day on the street, freedom was becoming more precious and real. Quinpool Road in Halifax, Nova Scotia, was filled with the sounds of a Sunday evening in the city. It was music to my ears.

Two weeks earlier, I had been released to a halfway house. Life was full except for one small detail. I still had not found a place to worship the One who had set me free on the inside.

My walk came to a temporary halt at a red light. The smell of free air and the sound of traffic roaring by were invigorating. As I waited for the light to turn, I realized there was a large church beside me. This place looked familiar. I walked over to the sign posted on the church wall and read, "West End United Baptist Church, Services at 11:00 a.m. & 7:00 p.m."

I glanced at my watch. It was about 6:30 p.m. I pondered my next move. *Should I go in?*

A memory from the past prodded me toward the door. I

---

[18] Some translations prefer to use the literal interpretation of the Hebrew word *qol* "voice of" instead of an interjection "Listen". See page 107 of *Genesis 1-15: Word Biblical Commentary*, by Gordon J Wenham.

climbed up the steps and gently opened the door, walking into the entryway of the church. I chose a seat on the main floor near the back. As I sat down, I took in the sanctuary, noticing the balcony on the left.

Yes, this place was very familiar. The last time I had been here was over a year ago. It had been a very sad occasion, yet one which God used to touch my life in a way I never dreamed possible.

My thoughts drifted back to the events that led to my entering this beautifully-crafted house of worship for the first time, events that had begun in prison.

· · ·

I sat looking around the small cell I had come to know as home. Breakfast was the usual fare. My morning devotions were completed, and I sat patiently in my work boots and prison green uniform waiting for the familiar voice of authority to holler down the range, "Time for work!"

The last year had been a struggle. Not so much because of the place I lived in, but because of the calling I felt God placing on my life, a call to ministry. At first, I thought it was a silly idea that would pass. But it stuck. In fact, it became more persistent with time.

I suppose most people who are called into ministry feel honoured to receive such a special summons from the Master. Well, I didn't. Instead, apprehension was building right alongside the call. It took the form of a question that would not go away, a question that was growing louder and more persistent than the call itself. "How would the Christian community on the outside react to an ex-con in their midst, especially one who felt called to ministry?"

"Time for work!" blared over the speaker system. I lifted

myself off the bed and stepped out of my cell, closing the steel door behind me as I began walking down the range. I was just about to clear the range barrier when suddenly a name caught my attention.

Someone was listening to the morning news on the radio. The commentator's voice drifted out of the cell. "The body of Rev. Gerry Fuller was found…"

Hitting a brick wall would not have stopped me faster. All my attention focused on the commentator's voice as they continued, "Police believe he was murdered by…"

My heart missed a couple of beats. My head began to spin. *It can't be,* I thought. *Not Gerry! Please, God, no!*

I walked out into the yard, sure I had heard it wrong. But as the day wore on and I talked with others, my worst fears were confirmed. As I had pieced my life back together, after my encounter with the abyss, Gerry had become a friend, a brother in Christ, someone I had come to know and deeply respect. Now he was dead…murdered.

The following day brought with it the same old routine, although the routine seemed much heavier. The call to work came, and I trudged my way up to the main gate of the prison. I was working outside the fence on a work crew. As I stood at the main gate awaiting clearance, the gate slowly ground open, then slammed shut again as Hugh strolled in for his work day. He was the summer chaplain at the prison that year.

I'm not sure what it was, perhaps my eyes, my face, or the way I was standing, but Hugh instantly recognized the weight I was carrying. I don't remember much of our conversation, only Hugh's gentle question. "Hank, do you want to go to Gerry's funeral?"

I thought for a moment, and then with a heavy heart, I replied, "Sure."

"Don't worry about it," he said. "I'll take care of it."

The moment the words left my mouth I regretted letting them escape. Unfortunately, before I could say anything, Hugh was gone through the next gate.

As I walked out through the gate, my stomach tightened. *What in the world have I done?* I thought. *There will be prison volunteers there who will know me! A convicted murderer, at the funeral of someone just murdered!*

I pushed aside the rising fear and tried not to think about the funeral for the rest of the day.

Two days later, I found myself in the front seat of a white Volkswagen racing toward Halifax, with Hugh at the wheel. Those two days had brought little relief for my anxiety. As we drew closer to Halifax, the fear grew more intense.

By the time we arrived at the church, my chest felt as if two huge hands were squeezing the life out of me. The dull headache which had awoken me that morning was now a jackhammer.

It took superhuman effort to step from the car and up the steps into the church. Every fibre of my body wanted to run. I nudged Hugh to go upstairs to the balcony overlooking the main sanctuary. My hope was that dissolving into a crowd, far from the front of the church, would ease the unrelenting pressure of being there.

Hugh and I climbed the stairs to the second floor and found seats at the front of the left balcony. As the service began, Gerry's wife, Barb, and their children were guided to the front pew of the church.

Barb had been part of a group of volunteers who attended the Kairos Marathon Encounter sessions at the prison Chapel. Looking down on her, now a widow, who had just lost her husband to murder, and her children who had been left fatherless by an utterly senseless act of violence…sometimes, the mirror God holds up to our conscience is painfully penetrating.

I took a deep breath, closed my eyes, wrestling to stay in

control of powerful emotions swirling deep within me. I didn't hear much of the service. I was lost in a world of pain, guilt, and reckoning with my own dark past.

Then, near the end of the service, Gerry's voice sprang from the speaker system. They had chosen to play a recording of one of his sermons. His voice and passion for the Lord reverberated through the sanctuary, reassuring me I had reason for being there. Gerry, in his own unique way, had touched my life with that passion. For the first time since I had heard of his death, tears rolled down my face.

The service ended. I now had to figure out a way to leave the building without being noticed.

I made it downstairs. Stepping into the front area of the church, I turned a corner. Suddenly, I was face to face with the one person I had feared meeting most.

Standing no more than ten feet in front of me was Barb. She looked straight at me. I froze. I couldn't think. My mind scrambled to put up all the emotional armour I could muster, ready for whatever might happen.

Her eyes revealed more pain than I could fathom. She put her arms around me, gave me a gentle hug and said, "Hank, it's really good to have you here."

She left as quickly as she came, leaving me standing there, stunned.

How? I thought. *How could a woman who had just lost her husband through the violent act of murder come and hug a man who had caused the same kind of pain in someone else's life?*

Before I could answer myself, I found Eric, a good friend of Gerry's, standing in front of me with his hand outstretched.

I reached out and took his hand. "Hank. It's good to have you here."

Person after person walked up and greeted me with warmth and openness. Not a single negative comment was flung my way.

As I left the church that afternoon to return to prison, it began to dawn on me that God had answered my question.

• • •

The faint echo of the last hymn penetrated my reflections. I stood up and bowed my head as the pastor closed the evening service. With people moving out of the sanctuary, I found myself wanting to stay a little longer.

Just as I was about to sit down again, I noticed a man approaching. I straightened up and took hold of his outstretched hand.

A warm smile crossed his face. "Hi. My name is Grant. Welcome to West End."

As we exchanged a firm handshake, I knew I had found a place to fellowship. And God again was quietly affirming His call on my life.

The Road Less Travelled

There is a journey some convicts travel, either by choice or driven by forces of remorse, faith, and pain. The path moves through the depths of a person's being into caverns known only to them and God. It is there that ghosts of the past linger, like a dark mist waiting to roar back to life when you least desire to encounter them.

Their power does not exist in the events they play out, or in the eruption of emotions they contain. Their force is in the mirror they craft, throwing back an image of you, crashing through any self-made facade.

"This is you," they say. "You were there. You chose to be there. You chose to act. You chose to inflict pain, hurt, humiliation, death on another person solely for your own gain and pleasure."

On the night of my crime, as my accomplice began ransacking the house we broke into, I tied up the man who was there. "You're not going to kill me, are you?" he asked.

"Of course not," I replied. It was the last words we spoke. I remember the quiver in his voice, blood oozing down his face from the gash on the side of his head, and my utter indifference to his fear.

An hour later he was dead.

Who was I? What kind of person would do that? the mirror informed me.

Ghosts are an apt way to describe these memories. There is a dark, destabilizing, haunting quality about them. They have the ability to tear at your sanity, leaving internal chaos as they drift through your thoughts. Unbeckoned, unwanted, they charge into your conscience, demanding an audience. They are the voice of God challenging us to "Listen!"—a signal that there are things in life to face, things no one wants to face about themselves.

Who wants to take a journey where the course is one of exposing the darkest parts of you? It is no wonder many avoid even starting down this path.

However, the man in prison who proclaims a new faith in Jesus Christ will sooner or later have to embark on this difficult road of self-discovery. It is not an option. When it is treated as one, the process of change stalls. Sooner or later, the Holy Spirit will prod you to the door. To underscore this reality, I would like to introduce you to a quote I came across some time ago. Before I share it, let me also introduce the man who wrote it, Rod Carter.

I met Rod when I first began moving in chaplaincy circles. We had an instant connection. He had served time in Kingston Penitentiary for manslaughter and eventually obtained a pardon. Rod was ordained to ministry in 1984 with the United Church of Canada. He went on to serve as a pastor in the First Nation communities of Saddle Lake and Good Lake, Alberta. In 1990, he began work with the Correctional Service of Canada as a Chaplain at Joyceville Institution. Eventually, he was appointed Regional Chaplain for the Ontario Region. Rod was seconded in 2000 to Queens School of Religion as the Director of the Restorative Justice Program until 2010 when he passed away.

Rod was as down to earth as a person could be. He understood the landscape of change better than most. Not only had he lived it, but he taught it, impacting many lives in the process.

He wrote:

> A prison Chaplain is ever alert to fanaticism, the dispensation of cheap grace and religious addiction. Rehabilitation only comes through honesty and brutal self-examination. The enemy is within and that's where the 180-degree turn begins. That's why Dr. Jekyll and Mr. Hyde still reads well in a prison cell. Restoration involves full admission of wrongdoing, acknowledgement of who was damaged by our crime, restitution where possible, recognition of our shadow side and its capacity for destruction and getting in touch with our emotions. This can only be achieved if trust is established because the pain is so intense, the fury so alive and crust around feelings so hardened.[19]

---

[19] From an article he wrote for *The United Church Observer*, called "Days of diamonds, days of stone", found on page 29-30, September 1996.

Rod's words helped me appreciate that my voice is not alone in proclaiming the need for the Christian convict to travel this road, or for that matter, any person in prison who declares they are changing.

A Journey Begins

Dr. Charlie Taylor led numerous Clinical Pastoral Education Units at Springhill Institution while I was still serving time there.[20] I had the privilege of working in the Chapel as a cleaner for a number of years, which meant, for a good portion of the summers I occupied that position, I got to participate in Charlie's morning devotionals.

There were usually six to eight student chaplains who would take the program. They would gather in a circle, and Charlie always invited me and the other Chapel cleaner, also a lifer, to join them.

On one particular morning, Rev. Pierre Allard was the guest for the day. Pierre was a chaplain and the Regional Chaplain for the Atlantic region. He would go on to become the Head of federal prison chaplaincy in Canada. Neither I nor the other Chapel cleaner knew much about Pierre, except that he was a deeply committed, enthusiastic man of faith.

Pierre began the morning devotion by talking about his family and how one of his brothers went in the opposite direction from himself. His brother became involved in organized crime and ended up paying for it with his life. He was discovered in a field, executed.

---

[20] For more information on Clinical Pastoral Education Units in Canada, the Canadian Association for Spiritual Care offers the following website: https://spiritualcare.ca/education_home/cpe-units/

Pierre recounted how they prayed for his brother regularly and tried everything possible to draw him out of the lifestyle he had chosen. His murder was devastating for Pierre.

Through much prayer and questioning, a deeply comforting insight began to emerge. Even though Pierre didn't know what the last minutes of his brother's life had been, he was assured that even in those last desperate moments God was present with his brother.

I sat there in the circle, surrounded by prison chaplains, facing my fellow Chapel cleaner. We looked at each other. The expression on his face let me know he was as shaken as I.

A time of sharing followed. Neither one of us was able to formulate a coherent response. We were both lost in our own thoughts. Unlike Pierre and the other chaplains, neither of us were drawing comfort from the devotion. Conviction, shame, regret, and pain was rising from deep within me. I wanted so much to say, "I'm sorry," but it sounded hollow, empty, too little too late. I said nothing.

The devotional came to a close. Charlie and Pierre started the morning session while the other cleaner and I went back to work. We didn't say much to each other. There was nothing to say. We were each travelling our own hidden journey.

That experience hung heavy with me as one question whirled through my mind: *How could a man whose brother was murdered possibly work in these places?*

More troubling though, was the recognition that on that night, as I tied up my victim, and left him to ponder his fate, God was with him. There was no comfort in that thought, just more conviction, an agonizing recognition that in midst of all the darkness I embraced, God was present taking care of a man whom I, with callous indifference, took part in murdering.

Pierre's devotion was the beginning of my hidden journey, a

journey that has continued through to the present and moves into the future.

It is difficult to describe this journey. One way I have tried, is to imagine myself standing on an ocean shoreline facing east. It is dark, and I am just a few hundred feet back from the water. As the sun begins to emerge over the horizon, beautiful rays of light start to dance off the water, revealing gentle waves touching the shore. The emerging light warms my face. It is a good place to be.

I can't see much. There is still a hazy darkness hanging in the air. Slowly, as the sun rises further, the shoreline comes into view. There is something on the shore, but it is hard to make out. I strain to see it.

As the light rises, a shattered building emerges from the shadows. A small knot begins to form in my stomach. There is a connection between this shattered building and me, but I am not sure what it is. The sun continues to rise with light revealing more destruction. With more light comes more destruction. House after house lie in ruin all around me.

Then, as the light reveals my hands, I see they are holding the tools of destruction. The knot in my stomach is now an immense inner pain as I realize I was responsible for this.

When a person comes to faith in Jesus Christ, the Holy Spirit begins His amazing work. Consider the light of the sun in the above metaphor as the power of the Holy Spirit beginning to work in a person's life. The brighter it shines, the more it uncovers. The image of numerous destroyed homes is the reality that our crime has impacted not only our victim, but their family, their friends, their community, our family, our friends, our community.

This slow, gradual awakening does not occur in a sudden flash of time. It is a slow process which moves forward in short bursts of semi-revelation, until the revelations add up to a much wider, profoundly honest perspective of our actions.

What began with Pierre's devotion has not stopped. It cannot stop. The more I see, the more is revealed, the more I am humbled; the more I grow in compassion and care for those around me.

Individuals who are truly transformed through their faith in Christ cannot ignore the hidden journey into the dark caverns where haunting memories reside. It is in these powerful encounters with our "shadow side and its capacity for destruction" that, strangely, new life begins to take shape, especially if we allow the Holy Spirit to work. We are humbled, broken down, fumbling to understand.

And there, in the midst of all that confusion, God's hand is at work, reshaping and rebuilding. It changes you. Life never looks the same again. Out of the brokenness in our lives and the brokenness we have caused in other lives, emerges a profound need to try and help wherever we can.

Some would suggest those of us who feel this way are simply trying to make amends. It goes far beyond trying to make amends. We start to see the world differently. Our deepest desires are transformed. We want our actions to be the direct opposite of what they have been.

The apostle Paul, a man who himself murdered (Acts 8:1), writes, "Anyone who has been stealing must steal no longer, but must work, doing something useful with their own hands, that they may have something to share with those in need." (Ephesians 4:28)

For those of us who have travelled down this road, Paul's words echo our driving passion. It can grip us with a force that will not let go.

A Good Man

Perhaps one of the most striking facets of walking my own hidden journey has been how I can relate to other men going through the same. One such event is etched in my memory, a heartfelt discussion with an inmate named Harvey.

It had been a tough conversation as we sat in the visiting area of the institution. He was back inside for a revocation after doing so well. He was staying clean, studying at university, reconnecting with friends and family. Then it all fell apart. The loneliness started to build. It was too much. Next came a friendly welcoming group, a beer, and then the downward slide began.

As we sat looking at each other, talking about his attempts to somehow give back, make atonement for the horrible things he had done, we talked about the burden we both carried, the reality that nothing brings back the dead. There is no way to fix it. We just need to learn to live with it.

I looked at him and just made a statement of fact. I didn't know it would hit so deep. "Harvey, you're a good man. Your heart longs to make amends. You are a good man."

The tears slowly slid down his face, a face etched with years of journeying through gangs and death.

We sat in quietness. My heart ached to give a magic moment of healing. I had none. All I had to offer was to be present, encouraging him as he wrestled to find the path that would help him heal, and learn to live with the reality of the void he had left in the lives of others.

A Teacher's Story

When I started as a Pastor in rural Nova Scotia, I anticipated there would be some resistance to having a former convict for a pastor.[21] To my surprise there was little, except from one member. Beryl was a retired teacher, who had been sexually assaulted a few years prior to my coming to the pastorate. She voted against my call to the parish.

One Sunday afternoon, a church deacon approached me. "Hank, I think it might be a good idea if you were to visit with Beryl. She voted against your coming to the pastorate. You know she was assaulted?"

"Yes. I had planned to go and talk with her."

I was completely unprepared for what he said next. "You know, she has never been the same since."

I was shocked with how matter-of-fact his statement came out, but like a good pastor, who was new to the churches, I kept my own counsel.

Her house sat near the corner of two main roads. It was a beautiful old home surrounded by trees, the kind of place that has a nice country charm but looks like it could use some work.

I had called before going over. Beryl greeted me at the door, ushered me into the kitchen, and we sat down. Never underestimate the power of an elderly retired teacher. With steely eyes she looked at me over a steaming cup of tea. "I voted against you coming here. Nothing personal."

There was a moment of silence. "I understand, Beryl."

What followed was a very personal conversation with a few direct questions about my life. Suffice it to say she invited me back for tea. As I was about to leave, she commented her stove wasn't working that well. It was an old-wood-oil-cooktop combination and the carburetor on the back of it was not

---

[21] I will always be thankful for the people of North Brookfield, South Brookfield, Westfield, and New Elm who chose to accept Linda, the children, and I into their world.

working. The carburetor controls the flow of fuel into the stove. She was having trouble getting someone to fix it.

Before I even realized it, the words were out of my mouth. "You know, Beryl, I am pretty mechanical. I can come have a look at it."

She eyed me again with that steely gaze. "Okay."

The following Saturday I arrived, tools in hand, and spent a couple of hours tearing the carburetor apart, cleaning it and then putting it back together. Within a short period of time, warm heat was flowing through the kitchen.

"A cup of tea?"

"Sure, Beryl." We sat down for another conversation.

Pastors aren't supposed to have favourites. I broke the rule. Beryl became a regular on my visiting schedule. If I stretched out the time between visits a little too long, well, I heard about it. What began as a furnace fix turned into locks that needed repairing, a door that wasn't closing properly, plumbing repairs, a tap here, a plugged drain there, a frozen pipe, small jobs that in the country were difficult to get fixed.

I even grabbed our neighbour Roddy for a couple of jobs. "Roddy, I need some help fixing a leak on Beryl's roof."

"Ah, Hank, I'm kind of busy right now."

"Roddy, not to lay a guilt trip on you, but it is your Pastor asking." He shuffled off to get his tools and we fixed a leaky roof.

For six years Beryl and I visited. Our connection grew. I learned that the individual who assaulted her was a former student, whose family lived only a few houses down the road. I visited with the family, learning about their pain and struggle. As I got to know the people in the community, the immense damage that radiated out from the assault slowly emerged.

One afternoon, as we sat for tea, Beryl looked at me. "You have never asked what happened to me. Would you like to know?"

"Yes, I would, Beryl."

I remember the room, the old furniture, light streaming in through the window. I remember her soft voice as she described being sexually assaulted for hours. Her attacker finally left, but not before tying her hands to a door handle. For two days she remained there, naked, left to die. She recounted her last few minutes as death approached. Her spirit was about to leave her body, when she heard a voice from downstairs. Someone had come to check on her.

Quietly she said, "I guess God still had something for me to do."

We sat together in silence, as warm sunlight flickered through the lace curtains. She smiled as I looked at her and we continued our conversation. It would not be the last time Beryl and I talked about God, her purpose in life, and what death looked like.

A couple of years later, Linda, our children, and I left congregational ministry and I moved into prison chaplaincy. Our family connection with Beryl continued. Each year we would send her a Christmas card, occasionally with an updated family picture. Each year she wrote back, sharing the local news.

The words on one such card sent me for a quiet walk. She wrote:

"Thank you for the family picture you sent. You are a very special person."

Beryl passed away on June 30, 2018 at the age of 97. I never did tell her how much she gave to me in our relationship. Maybe one day I will have the chance. Her courage, her acceptance, her willingness to let an ex-con into her life—it was profoundly healing on my hidden journey. I hope I too may have brought her a measure of healing.

A Cloud of Witnesses

Gerry Fuller's funeral marked a turning point in my personal hidden journey. I was in the midst of the Christian community on the street, facing my past and looking at the future. There was no getting away, nowhere to hide. I had to "listen" (Genesis 4:10). Right in front of me was the impact of a murder staring back at me as I sat in the balcony. It was an overwhelming, desolate, numbing place to be.

Yet, into that wasteland of utter emptiness poured the most miraculous of God's power, the ultimate gift of the Christian faith: grace. Gerry's words were bouncing out of heaven into my life, and Barb's embrace…

In that experience I began to catch a glimpse of what the writer in Hebrews was getting at when he wrote, "Therefore, since we are surrounded by such a great cloud of witnesses, let us throw off everything that hinders and the sin that so easily entangles, and let us run with perseverance the race marked out for us." (Hebrews 12:1)

A change was occurring. The haunting echoes of my past actions were still there, but there was a transformation underway. They didn't have the death grip they once had. Instead, they were becoming firm reminders, anchors in humility, resonating with the Apostle Paul's words written long after his conversion: "Christ Jesus came into the world to save sinners—of whom I am the worst." (1 Timothy 1:15b)

As I moved into prison chaplaincy, there was a cloud of witnesses that surrounded my interactions with all whom I met. Gerry's great warmth, Barb's gentle hug, Beryl's brokenness, Pierre's pain and forgiveness, Charlie and Charlotte's unconditional love. I could name more.

The hidden journey doesn't end. It continues to unfold.

Even today, there are moments of deep regret. That will never change. Yet, it has become clear that the hidden journey need not destroy if you are guided by wise counsellors and the work of the Holy Spirit. In fact, it can transform your life.

5. Primum non Nocere

And now I will show you the most excellent way.
If I speak in the tongues of men and of angels, but have not love,
I am a resounding gong or a clanging cymbal.
If I have the gift of prophecy and can fathom all mysteries
and all knowledge, and if I have faith that can move mountains,
but have not love I am nothing. If I give all I possess to the poor
and surrender my body to the flames, but have not love,
I gain nothing.
(I Corinthians 13:1–3)

It was the spring of 2014. Linda, our two grown children, Isaac and Teresa, along with a number of other family members, had gathered at a favourite restaurant in downtown Winnipeg. As the waiter approached our table, she could see we were in jovial mood and asked, "So what are we celebrating today?"

Someone piped up, "Well, we are celebrating Hank receiving his doctorate."

"So, what kind of medical doctor are you going to be?"

I explained I had just earned a Doctor of Ministry degree. A puzzled look crossed her face as she tried to unravel what the terms "doctor" and "ministry" could possibly have in common.

Without a moment's hesitation my beautiful daughter said, "He is going to be a doctor of the soul."

This only added to the perplexed expression crossing the waiter's face as she walked away to get our order of drinks. It was a profoundly humbling moment. Teresa had spoken those words with deep conviction and respect.

I share the above moment because Teresa's perspective—that I was now a "doctor of the soul"—provides a helpful way to begin a discussion about a principle I would offer to those who journey alongside men and women in prison: *primum non nocere*—"above all, do not harm".

Although there is some debate about the exact origin of this phrase, it has become a central axiom in the medical profession.[22] I would contend it should be a central axiom for those in the Christian community who choose to minister in prisons.

This may seem a moot point. After all, prison ministry is supposed to be about reducing harm. Surely chaplains and volunteers don't need a reminder to do no harm.

Perhaps they do.

Honour

We always had an interesting assortment of personalities gracing our Stony Mountain Chapel space. Most of them would never steal from us, but then, this was a prison, and a prison does house thieves. Sure enough, now and then someone would feel the urge to relieve the Chapel of its sugar or whitener.

To address the issue, we would occasionally remind the men that stealing the condiments was not helpful because somebody had to pay for them. Along with this reminder, we would keep a vigilant eye on the whitener and sugar, which were placed by the

---

[22] Further discussion on this can be found in the article "Origin of Uses of Primum Non Nocere: Above All, Do Not Harm!" by C. Smith.

coffee urn. This was not always an easy task with fifty people milling around and a few vying for your attention.

As a final line of defence, we decided to only put a small quantity out at a time. If anything, it would cut our losses and reinforce the reality that if someone stole the items, the containers would remain empty for a while. Along with Bo, the Roman Catholic Chaplain who ran the Chapel with me, we had come to the conclusion this was part of the cost of doing business. Coffee could be eliminated, but that would detract from the time of fellowship.

On one particular evening, the sugar bowl was emptying very quickly.

It had been a good service. Including volunteers, we had about fifty people in the Chapel. As was our custom at the end of the service, we moved the coffee urn out into the area at the back of the Chapel. People could grab a coffee and move back into the sanctuary area to mingle and visit.

The sugar disappeared several times. Sunny, one of the inmates, wandered over for a coffee, only to discover the thief had struck yet again. Clearly, a serial sugar thief was on the loose. He picked up the bowl and walked over to a new chaplain I was training. The chaplain had arrived at the institution just a couple of months earlier. She was still acclimatizing to the new world in which she found herself. In a respectful manner, Sunny asked the chaplain for more sugar. I could tell she was getting frustrated at having to fill the sugar so many times tonight.

Looking at him squarely, the chaplain shot back, "Why should I get more sugar for you? You people are always stealing it!"

I froze. My blood pressure shot up. I stood there, stunned, ready for Sunny to let her have it verbally.

He looked hurt as he spoke. "Hey. That's unfair. I didn't

steal any sugar." Glancing in my direction he added, "Hank, tell her she is wrong."

My words snapped out with more force than intended. "That is unfair. You can't be judging people like that." The chaplain walked away to get sugar, and Sunny went to find a chair to sit down in.

Others standing around had watched it all unfold. I waited about ten minutes to let the tension level in the area ease off. It was high because there was a deeper disturbing layer to the exchange that had occurred. The new chaplain was white. Sunny was Indigenous. There was no question in my mind how "you people" was understood.

I went over and sat down beside Sunny. By then he had gotten his coffee and was sitting by himself. I apologized and thanked him for holding his cool in a situation that could have turned ugly in seconds.

"She had no right to say that," he stated again.

"I know. It won't happen again," I assured him.

We sat there for a few minutes sharing a joke or two. Sunny had a wonderful sense of humour. He had been coming to Chapel off and on over the last few months. He was wrestling with both personal and spiritual issues in his life.

Our Chapel time came to an end. I shook Sunny's hand as he left. I hoped the incident would not stop him from coming to Chapel.

Two weeks later a request form arrived on my desk. In the subject line, Sunny wrote: *Mother Dying*. It continued, *I can't sleep. I think about my Mom and other stuff in my life too much. I think it would help to talk to a chaplain about these things.*

I called Sunny down and we met in my office for over an hour. During that time, he poured out his heart, and I got a glimpse of the struggles he had, until now, held in.

He started by detailing his earlier life of abuse, how he ended up in foster care, and going through more than thirty foster placements until a Mennonite family took him in and legally adopted him. Life had been good, but as he entered his teenage years things began to spiral out of control. His adopted parents were able to get him into Teen Challenge twice. The first time he lasted four days. The second time he stayed for seven months. Afterwards, Sunny was able to stay sober for a couple of years. He connected with Youth With A Mission, a Christian organization that helps youth channel their energies and desires into serving others through different projects around the world.

It didn't last. Sunny eventually found himself in trouble again and this time ended up serving federal time. While on the street, he made connections with one of the gangs prevalent in both Stony Mountain Institution and in the community. When he arrived at the prison, the pressure was on to join the gang. He was useful, strong, big, with martial arts training. Just what a gang needed—good muscle. He joined.

Sunny was not happy with his decision. In time, he started coming to Chapel and met a couple of men who were very committed to living out their newfound faith. This is the Sunny I first met.

But there was still a lot more to Sunny's story, as his next words revealed.

One of the men he bonded with in Chapel was another inmate, Harold. He played a key role in Sunny returning to faith in God. He also challenged Sunny on the reality that he needed to cut his connections with the gang if he was truly recommitting his life to Christ. As he put it, using Jesus' words, "No one can serve two masters." (Matthew 6:24)

For Sunny, those words cut deep. He decided Harold was right. The ties had to be broken.

But there was a problem. Cutting ties would mean a deboarding—a beating by the gang.

Sunny and Harold talked often. They prayed about the situation and Sunny decided it was time. His biggest concern— one Harold was well aware of because he had been involved with street gangs—was that sometimes a de-boarding resulted in death. In fact, both knew of incidents where this had occurred. Harold's response to this concern was, "Well, if that happens, you at least know where you are going—home."

The decision was made. One evening during exercise, Sunny went to the gym—in his words, "Not knowing if I was going to live or die."

He stepped into the gym and went up to a group of leading gang members. "Guys, I have recommitted my life to God. I want out."

They laughed at him. "You're joking, right?"

"No, this is for real."

"You know what that means?"

"Yeah, I do."

"You're willing to go through that?"

"Yeah."

"Okay."

The gang leadership moved over to the back of the gym to discuss what to do. Soon, they returned. "Okay, into the washroom now."

They chose the washroom in the gym for these kinds of "events" because there are no cameras to monitor activity. Sunny was escorted over to the washroom by a number of gang members. He stepped into the washroom, and three men were sent in with him along with a timekeeper. He removed the jewellery he was wearing.

The timekeeper looked at him. "Two minutes," he said. He started the stopwatch. "Now!"

Sunny dropped after the first hard punch and for the next two minutes, three men beat him. They kicked, punched, and stomped on him for two whole minutes. Three strong, young men can do a great deal of damage to another human being in two minutes. Sunny's friends had to carry him back to his cell without being noticed by staff.

The de-boarding crew did their job well. As Sunny put it, "They messed me up good. I was bleeding out of my ears. I am sure I was bleeding internally. I spent the next week in bed."

I personally know they did a good job. I remember Sunny coming to Chapel a couple of weeks after the incident, very bruised up. Wise chaplains know it is best not to ask certain questions. You are only going to get a smart response like, "Walked into a door."

For those not schooled in the world of gangs and prison you are probably thinking, "This is crazy. Why didn't he run and get protection from staff?" A nice idea, but not always a safe option. The gang he belonged to was also active on the street. Going to "protection" would simply have put a target on his back.[23] And actually, one of his bigger concerns at that point was if he went to protection, it would have limited his access to Chapel.

After he finished sharing his full story, we sat in silence. Finally, Sunny lowered his head. "I try, you know, but I am not sure I am much of a Christian."

That moment is seared into my memory. I sat there with a young man who had been physically, emotionally, and spiritually bounced around most of his life, the tattoos on his arms, face, and hands etching out his painful struggle to find his real identity. All this, wrapped in a life full of personal failures and scarring baggage.

---

[23] Institutions sometimes have special units set aside for individuals who have difficulties in the General Population. Although different names are assigned to these units, they are normally called Protective Custody Units among frontline staff and inmates, thus the term "protection".

There are Christians in the community who can't even be bothered to roll out of bed on a Sunday morning to attend church. Yet Sunny was willing to risk it all to stay true to his faith commitment and not lose full access to the Chapel.

This was the heart of the man who the new chaplain accused of stealing in front of peers and volunteers. It is nothing short of a miracle that Sunny took another risk and reached out to talk with me, another chaplain.

"Sunny," I said to him, "God honours those who honour him."

Scared Straight?

Some chaplains can be very judgemental—in other words, blind. This capacity for judging others has its roots in the twin vices of arrogance and ignorance.

Arrogance is rooted in a false sense of superiority. Ignorance in this case comes from not knowing about what goes on in a prison, how it functions, and what the inhabitants are really like. And while the story of Sunny and my trainee chaplain stands out as an example of this, it is far from being the most glaring.

I'll never forget the night I was asked to facilitate a service for an evangelist from a well-known American ministry. He came highly recommended by a couple of other chaplains and had been all over the United States and Africa speaking in prisons.

The evangelist got up to speak. What followed is a scene that sealed the fate of any other evangelistic requests I received while I was chaplain. Thrusting his fists into the air as if striking out at some unknown assailant, he shouted at the top of his lungs. Later I heard a complaint from the medical wing which is right beside the Chapel—he was that loud.

Face turning red, eyes filled with rage, twisting and turning, he demanded men make a commitment of faith. For twenty minutes, this display of rage went on. I was stunned. The men were stunned. No one came forward.

The following day, one of the men who had been at the service dropped by the Chapel to speak with me. Don had spent over twenty years in and out of prison. He had seen or been a part of just about anything you can imagine going on in a prison—fights, stabbings, riots. His youth was filled with the chaos of physical and sexual abuse. Drugs were his escape.

As he sat in my office reflecting on the experience of the prior night, Don spoke words that have hung with me ever since. "I came to see you today because last night, sitting in the Chapel, a place where I like to come and feel safe, I felt completely verbally abused."

Don and I had a good relationship, one that had encompassed more than a few journeys into the deep waters of his troubled life. He was disappointed I had allowed this evangelist to be there.

He was right. I should have known better. At the very least, I should have shut him down. For Don and no doubt a few other men in Chapel that night, what they saw and heard were echoes of the violent abuse they had endured as children.

I apologized. Combined, arrogance and ignorance are potent destructive forces.

Contrast

Allow me to contrast the two stories I have just shared with the words of the prophet Isaiah foretelling the nature of the Messiah:

Here is my servant, whom I uphold,
my chosen one in whom I delight;
I will put my Spirit on him
and he will bring justice to the nations.
He will not shout or cry out,
or raise his voice in the streets.
A bruised reed he will not break,
and a smoldering wick he will not snuff out.
(Isaiah 42:1-3)

Many who have entered the prison system, including myself, are not drawn to loud, judgemental voices. Instead, what drew us to faith and moved us forward were individuals who exuded in word and deed the truth, "Above all, do not harm." We sensed— we knew— these people would not break a bruised reed or snuff out a smoldering wick. We found a gentle compassion, an open heart, a willingness to engage with care, and an incredible ability to speak difficult truth in love.

I have come to believe this axiom is one of the fundamental principles that sets prison chaplaincy apart from other ministries. In a world where there are so many damaged and broken lives, this philosophy needs to be lived out as prison chaplains work with inmates, families, staff, victims, and other chaplains, no matter their faith tradition. Without it, you can perform the tasks of a prison chaplain, but for the most part you will be no more than a "resounding gong or a clanging cymbal". (1 Corinthians 13:1)

If my reflections thus far are conjuring up a saintly, holy chaplain, incapable of anger or offence, let me assure you that is not the model I am presenting. If we explore what is laid out in Scripture, we find Jesus quite capable of physically clearing the temple (John 2:12-16), calling religious leaders white washed tombs (Matthew 23:27) who make a convert "twice as much a son of hell as yourselves" (Matthew 23:15), and rebuking even his closest disciples with blunt power—"Get behind me, Satan!" (Mark 8:33)

Jesus was not a docile holy man. His life embraced both a profound compassionate care, one incapable of breaking a bruised reed, as well as a bedrock conviction to challenge when necessary, no matter the person or position they held.

These two elements define prison chaplaincy. What makes a prison chaplain effective is their ability to balance them.

This balance may appear an impossible task for some, but as with so much regarding ministry, if one is willing to set aside their arrogance and be open to dispelling their ignorance, doors of ministry open up that never existed before.

"That"

I was wrapping up ministry in Atlantic Institution in Renous, New Brunswick. During my last week, I was training a new chaplain. We were just returning from a walk on the segregation unit.

As I was about to open the Chapel door, located off one of the main hallways, Kelly came over. She had just been at Health Care, which was right across from the Chapel. Kelly was transgender. As I turned to greet her, I caught the expression on the new chaplain's face. He was taken aback by her appearance and presence in a maximum-security prison. She had long, flowing black hair, a strong yet gentle face, tight shirt and jeans on, along with all the feminine features that left no mistake about her identity.

"Hank, I need to talk to you for a minute," she said.

"Okay. What's up?"

What followed was a ten-minute conversation in the hallway, as she expressed her present fears and worries. Her partner was in segregation. She wanted to know if he was okay, and if I knew when he might be coming out of Seg and back to her range. She was worried, with good reason. The longer her partner stayed in Seg, the more of a target she became for someone to muscle her for sex. I assured her that Bob, her partner, was doing okay and promised to stop by and see him in the next few days. She thanked me for taking the time to talk and walked down the hallway.

I unlocked the door to the Chapel and stepped in with the new chaplain. As I closed and locked it behind us, he looked at me. "What do you do with that?" I of course knew what "that" was referring to.

"'That' is created in the image and likeness of God," I responded, "so, you will treat her just the same as anyone else here."

What the new chaplain didn't know at the time was some of Kelly's history. She had experienced a lot of violence, both in and out of prison. In Edmonton Max, where she had been housed on her last offence, she was forced to be a sex slave for one of the most violent men in the institution. Her freedom from him came at the hands of fellow inmates. They decided to end the life of her captor for completely unrelated reasons.

After I left Atlantic Institution, I began my chaplaincy at Stony Mountain Institution in Manitoba. About a year later, I received a phone call from the chaplain who had taken over at Atlantic.

"Hank, thought I would call and let you know, Kelly committed suicide. We had a service for her just a couple of weeks ago."

We had a long conversation about how things were unfolding at Atlantic. In the midst of the conversation, the chaplain talked about how his pastoral relationship with Kelly and her partner Bob had grown.

In fact, Bob was now coming to see him regularly, trying to deal with the loss.

Living "Above All, Do Not Harm"

Over the years, I have occasionally met highly-educated, highly-trained chaplains who did not do well in a prison. On the other hand, I have met individuals, who in the eyes of some of their peers, did not have enough education to be filling a chaplaincy role.

Yet these chaplains were profoundly effective, respected, and loved by both staff and inmate alike. They lived out the principle, "Above all, *do not harm.*"

There is a simple reason for this. Education alone does not train the heart and spirit. While education may assist, the core of training the heart and spirit is shaped via life experiences, personal reflection, and a vibrant relationship with the Creator who is working in our lives through the Holy Spirit.

That all said, formal education is a vital part of shaping effective prison chaplaincy. Education can improve the capacity of a chaplain to offer pastoral care. It can provide wisdom to navigate the difficult moral and ethical dilemmas that occasionally arise in a correctional environment. Education can challenge us in numerous ways, planting seeds for change and growth.

For over two thousand years, Christians have sought out others to help them walk the sometimes-difficult road of conversion and change. There is a deeply developed history of mentorship that flows through every church tradition in one form or another.

That tradition is very alive in a prison context. The ability to "above all, do not harm" is at the core of providing good mentorship and guidance to those seeking a way out of the darkness.

But "do not harm" extends well beyond the interactions a chaplain has with individuals serving time. It impacts every area of a prison chaplain's work with staff, volunteers, family, victims, other chaplains, different faith traditions, and the community. When this principle is not at work, the lingering distrust, suspicion, or outright hatred, which are an inevitable result, can undermine not only the work of the present chaplain, but also those chaplains who will follow.

When a chaplain chooses to belittle other faith traditions, undermine security protocols, bring contraband items in, openly battle with other chaplains, or engage in an affair with an inmate, the resulting harm to the work of chaplaincy can be devastating. Trust is lost. A shadow of suspicion hangs over the chaplaincy office. The capacity of the chaplain to speak into difficult situations is nullified as the word "hypocrite" drifts into conversations about the chaplain. Instead of conveying a pastoral caring presence, the title "chaplain" becomes devoid of any credibility.

Sadly, in my nine years as an inmate, fifteen years as a prison chaplain, five years training prison chaplains at Booth University College, and two years hiring and supervising chaplains for Kairos Pneuma Chaplaincy—which has allowed me to assess closely many chaplains to date—I have seen these types of situations play out more often than I'd like to admit.

Prison is a closed social environment. As a result, what you do in one part of the environment will quickly impact other parts. Most chaplains are unaware of the conversations that occur on the ranges, yards, offices, and meeting rooms that make up a prison, but they do. The inmate who arrives to talk or puts in a request to see you, has already asked some questions about your credibility. "Is he okay to talk with? Does he keep confidence?"

Staff are not any different. They, too, will confer with others. A Parole Officer dealing with a difficult situation and looking for some chaplaincy assistance will ask, "So, is this person okay? If I call them, will they respond? Will they follow-up? Do they take security seriously?"

Understanding "Love one another" in Prison

You might wonder why I have chosen to use the medical axiom, "Above all, do not harm" instead of Jesus' exhortation, "Love one another. As I have loved you, so you must love one another." (John 13:34) After all, everything that has been discussed so far is fundamentally powered by this commandment.

There is a problem with simply telling people to love one another in a correctional environment. It has to do with understanding how you can truly love and care for people in prison.

If you asked the two chaplains or the evangelist I mentioned earlier, "Are you expressing the love of Christ to men in prison?" they probably would have answered with an unequivocal, "Yes, of course we are. Otherwise, we would not be here."

All of us are capable of looking through the wrong lens when we try to interpret what it means to love another. More than one chaplain has found themselves alienated from staff because their lens of advocacy left no room for appreciating safety concerns.

Understanding Jesus' command to love others through a

harm reduction perspective helps us appreciate what loving another in a prison context actually looks like.

Let me provide a very simple example. A man arrives at the chaplain's office door after a worship service and pleads for a phone call to his partner on the street. He is being muscled by one of the gangs and has no money to put on his phone card, so he can't call her.

He makes a compelling case, tears and all. The chaplain has the ability to give the call. After all, what would be the harm? This looks like a situation that calls for some Christian compassion and love.

Yes, it does, but not in the way most would envision. What if there is a non-contact order in place? Can you trust the inmate to reveal that fact? What if the inmate is looking for a work-around in terms of trying to avoid having conversations with his partner recorded?

I once gave a call to a man who had just lost a family member. I first called the family to verify they would take his call. As soon as he got on the phone, he switched from English to another language. I was unable to understand a word he said. I knew something was up. I discovered he had a gambling addiction and was carrying a large debt with the local gangster bank. It turned out his parents, under duress, were a source of cash.

Not surprisingly, a couple of weeks later, guess who came looking for another call to his family? I refused.

Shortly after this naive moment, I changed the way I dealt with phone call requests. My response to any phone call request became: "Sure, no problem, but I will have to talk with your Parole Officer first." Not many came back to see if I had followed through.

The most loving act in this type of scenario is to refuse the phone call and then do your due diligence, appreciating others could potentially be harmed by what may appear a straight-forward act of compassion.

The principle, "Above all, do not harm," applies to every corner of prison chaplaincy. There are numerous times when a chaplain's actions and words, although meant to be loving, can turn out to be the opposite.

This means, in any given situation, determining a course of action that will do no harm can, on occasion, force a chaplain to weigh which option will create the least amount of harm for one party or the other, since no such option exists where no harm will be done at all. This is where we'll be turning next, as I share with you some of the most nuanced and difficult aspects of prison chaplaincy—but also, the most crucial, for it is here that I have found God's hand and agency at work in ways I could never have imagined.

6. Walking in the Dust

They asked each other,
"Were not our hearts burning within us while
he talked with us on the road and opened the Scriptures to us?"
(Luke 24:32)

Chaplains are called upon to perform many functions in an institution. Don Stoesz, who was a Protestant prison chaplain for over twenty-five years, has written extensively on these diverse roles. He divides prison ministry into over-lapping areas depending on the task at hand:

- Therapy/Socialization
- Private Office/Public Presence
- Activities Coordinator
- Faith Formation
- Religious Identity
- Programs
- Ritual[24]

Though I have focused mostly on principles and theology that help inform these different roles, there is one particular area of prison chaplaincy within Don's framework that is worth exploring: the individual interactions that occur within prison chaplaincy.

---

[24] From the book, *A Prison Chaplaincy Manual: The Canadian Context* by Donald Stoesz, pages 55-61.

A confusing element in these interactions has to do with the role of a chaplain. Are they engaged in pastoral counselling, spiritual direction, evangelism, social work, or are they acting as a life coach?

Chaplains sometimes default to the type of training they have received along their educational path. If they have completed a number of clinical pastoral education units, their leaning may be toward being more clinical. If entering prison ministry with no clinical training and limited pastoral education, chaplains may default to evangelism. If they have a spiritual direction background, their interactions with inmates will be based on giving guidance. While each of these disciplines is useful in a specific context, none of them singularly fit a prison chaplain's world.

A good example of this can be seen in a comment from an inmate. As we met in my office, we discussed personal concerns in his life he had been working through with another chaplain. It had not been a good experience for him. He remarked bluntly, "If I wanted therapy, I would go see a psychologist."

His words echoed my own experience as an inmate. One of the more disconcerting encounters I had was engaging with the occasional chaplain who wanted to be a therapist. I never quite knew what they were up to. I never felt that they were addressing the needs which I brought to them. Occasionally, they would use diagnostic tools[25] that quickly put me off. Neither I, nor that

---

[25] An example of a tool would be the Myers Briggs Type Indicator. Seldom do inmates understand whether such a tool has any validity or not, or in what context it is helpful. Added to this problem is where the collected information may be used in future. Sometimes one of the primary reasons inmates will talk with chaplains is because a chaplain is not a psychologist. Psychologists record information— information that ends up on a file—whereas chaplains do not.

inmate in my office, were looking for therapy in our connections with a chaplain.

The Emmaus Road

Although not speaking directly to a prison setting, Tilden Edward offers the term "Spiritual Friend", which is a better fit in a prison environment.[26] It probably comes closer than any other label to describing what men in prison seek when meeting with a chaplain. As uncomfortable as "friendship" terminology may be for the clinicians in the crowd, it more accurately reflects a scriptural definition of the individual work of prison chaplaincy, provided we understand this friendship is anchored within the spiritual dynamic of life.

After his resurrection Jesus declared to the disciples, "I no longer call you servants, because a servant does not know his master's business. Instead, I have called you friends, for everything that I learned from my Father I have made known to you." (John 15:15)

This perspective of spiritual friendship is not an easy path to navigate. Spiritual friendships in prison require firm clear boundaries defined by the safety and security concerns which are part of any institution.

How does the chaplain live out this "spiritual friendship" in practice? We need to move back into Scripture and explore a beautiful story found in the Gospel of Luke, chapter 24:13-35 to answer this question.

---

[26] From pages 1-9 of his book, *Spiritual Friend: Reclaiming the Gift of Spiritual Direction.*

¹³ Now that same day two of them were going to a village called Emmaus, about seven miles from Jerusalem. ¹⁴ They were talking with each other about everything that had happened. ¹⁵ As they talked and discussed these things with each other, Jesus himself came up and walked along with them; ¹⁶ but they were kept from recognizing him.

¹⁷ He asked them, "What are you discussing together as you walk along?"

They stood still, their faces downcast. ¹⁸ One of them, named Cleopas, asked him, "Are you the only one visiting Jerusalem who does not know the things that have happened there in these days?"

¹⁹ "What things?" he asked.

"About Jesus of Nazareth," they replied. "He was a prophet, powerful in word and deed before God and all the people. ²⁰ The chief priests and our rulers handed him over to be sentenced to death, and they crucified him; ²¹ but we had hoped that he was the one who was going to redeem Israel. And what is more, it is the third day since all this took place. ²² In addition, some of our women amazed us. They went to the tomb early this morning ²³ but didn't find his body. They came and told us that they had seen a vision of angels, who said he was alive. ²⁴ Then some of our companions went to the tomb and found it just as the women had said, but they did not see Jesus."

²⁵ He said to them, "How foolish you are, and how slow to believe all that the prophets

have spoken! ²⁶ Did not the Messiah have to suffer these things and then enter his glory?" ²⁷ And beginning with Moses and all the Prophets, he explained to them what was said in all the Scriptures concerning himself.

²⁸ As they approached the village to which they were going, Jesus continued on as if he were going farther. ²⁹ But they urged him strongly, "Stay with us, for it is nearly evening; the day is almost over." So he went in to stay with them.

³⁰ When he was at the table with them, he took bread, gave thanks, broke it and began to give it to them. ³¹ Then their eyes were opened and they recognized him, and he disappeared from their sight. ³² They asked each other, "Were not our hearts burning within us while he talked with us on the road and opened the Scriptures to us?"

³³ They got up and returned at once to Jerusalem. There they found the Eleven and those with them, assembled together ³⁴ and saying, "It is true! The Lord has risen and has appeared to Simon." ³⁵ Then the two told what had happened on the way, and how Jesus was recognized by them when he broke the bread.

"Jesus himself came up and walked along with them" (v.15)

I was doing a walk through the segregation unit at Atlantic Institution, moving from cell to cell. At each one, I stopped to talk with individuals through the side of the door. Although an awkward way to do business, it was the only way to communicate that day. The range was filled with the noise of men shouting and yelling obscenities. Frustrated men pounded doors that produced sharp, slamming sounds that reverberated down the range every minute or two.

Something had happened prior to my arrival to set them off. I could barely hear the men as I tried to talk with them. A number were cursing the world and anyone who came to their door—except, in most cases, the chaplain.

I considered leaving, despite having a few more cells to visit. The shockwave of slamming doors was starting to pound into my head. I thought better of it and stopped at the next door.

As I gazed through its small, thick glass window, I could see Wayne relentlessly pacing back and forth in the cell. He almost didn't hear when I greeted him—the noise from the rest of the range was now so loud it was almost deafening. He approached the window, tears rolling down his face. He was well over two hundred and fifty pounds, a big man. His shirt was off. Prison tattoos covered most of his body, along with numerous scars from past battles.

This wasn't my first time seeing him here. Segregation had been his home for some time. He just could not manage to function in the regular institutional population.

Tears flowed freely as he looked at me and mouthed the words, "I can't handle this anymore." I didn't say a word as I pressed my ear to the edge of his cell door. I let him talk. Frustration and pain sailed through the crack in the door, carried on a multitude of curses. Finally, he stopped.

I looked at him, then moved my mouth over to the edge of the door. "Would you like to pray?"

He nodded.

I stood there and prayed, surrounded by slamming doors,

men yelling obscenities at each other with the Lord's name intermittently tossed in for emphasis. Tears continued to stream down Wayne's face as I asked God to be present with him. No one knew. No one cared. No one could hear, except God, Wayne, and I. When we finished, I looked at him, put my hand up to the small window, and he did the same.

"Thanks."

A couple of weeks later I was back on the range. It was much quieter. I stopped at Wayne's cell. We looked at each other and smiled.

"How are you doing?" I asked.

"Okay."

We didn't need to say much more. On a quiet range, others are always listening. Best not to share too many personal thoughts. I went on to the next cell.

One of the reasons I am so drawn to the story of the Emmaus Road, is because of where it begins. In the opening verses we encounter two men whose entire world view had been shattered. They were lost. Hope was gone. The future was bleak. They were facing one of the most difficult points in any human being's existence—trying to rediscover hope for the future with nothing in the present to justify it.

Jesus "came up and walked along with them." He didn't walk behind them pushing them along. He didn't walk ahead of them pulling them along. He didn't appear in a vision overpowering them. He walked along with them, joining them on a dusty road.

The situations chaplains are called to address are not much different than what Jesus encountered on the Emmaus Road. It can be on a barely controlled Seg unit with a man slowly going insane, or meeting a newly-admitted inmate who has discovered his partner on the street has cleaned out the bank account, taken the kids, and said goodbye. Or, a man who has received word that the most important person in his life has died.

All these situations and many more share a common thread—some aspect of hope has slipped out of these men's grasp. Life in prison has just grown darker. Into these scenarios prison chaplains walk, in the dust of the road, not pushing men along with nonsense platitudes or walking ahead of them with an arrogant air of knowing better.

Wayne and I had formed an understanding as I walked with him. He wanted desperately to have some outside connection—something, someone—who carried hope. Numerous times, I didn't need to say very much to him. He knew I would be there to see him regularly and that I understood the unwritten rules of a Seg range.

What matters to Wayne and other men in prison who seek out a chaplain is whether or not their chaplain is going to walk alongside of them. What concerns them is whether their chaplain is going to judge them like the rest of the world has judged them. What is important to them is whether or not the chaplain is a person of compassion, whose words of care are backed up by the action of walking with them through their pain and brokenness.

If you say you will be back to visit someone in segregation and don't show up for three months, don't expect a warm reception. You are not walking with them.

It all sounds so simple. It is and it isn't. Over the years the most common complaint I heard regarding other chaplains is that the chaplain says they will do something—call somebody, visit them, call them down to the Chapel, provide a book or Bible—and then not fulfill the obligation. In a prison context this lack of follow-through communicates a clear message: "You weren't really that important, just another annoyance in my day."

Walking with men in prison is not easy. It requires time, energy, and commitment.

It doesn't require you to be perfect, though. I used to carry a small booklet with me and write down requests, no matter how small. The men got to know this habit well. If I didn't write the request down, they would remind me, "Hey, chaplain, you didn't write it down. You're going to forget if you don't put it down."

Though it would be great if I could remember the dozen requests on my plate at any time, and never forget a single one, the reality for me was that forgetting even one of them was worse than showing my fallibility. Instead of, "You weren't really important," it conveyed to the inmates I walked alongside, "I'm not perfect, but you are so important I've devoted a book to making sure this fact doesn't stop me from helping you."

"He explained to them what was said in all the Scriptures concerning him" (v. 27)

It seemed like an ordinary Sunday evening at Stony Mountain Institution. The inmates were just about to be released for Recreation. Soon there would be a number of men coming through to the Chapel.

It was my practice to stand near the door and shake everyone's hand as they came in. Often a few of the volunteers would follow suit.

As we stood shaking hands, it looked like we would have a good crowd that evening. There were men who didn't say a word. Others offered a polite hello. A few joked with us. Occasionally, there would be a hung head as someone back on a parole suspension sauntered in.

To all who came, we offered a warm welcome. It didn't matter who they were.

I let go of one hand, and as I prepared to grab the next, I

noticed the inmate it belonged to. He clasped my hand back firmly, a huge smile on his face as he said, "Remember me? You came to see me in Seg when I was here. You prayed with me there."

It took a couple of minutes as I rooted through my memory bank. I was in Seg often. "Jesse! You're back! That's great!"

Jesse was doing time for first degree murder, life and twenty-five. I'd visited him two years ago in Seg, before he was sent to the maximum-security prison. Under Canadian law, anyone sentenced to life must spend the first two years of their sentence in a Max.

After the service, we spent some time catching up. The first time I met Jesse in segregation, he was still on trial and never expected to be convicted. Money had bought him a top-notch lawyer. He thought life would go on as normal after he was acquitted. In the end, Jesse found himself sentenced to life and sitting in a segregation unit, awaiting transfer to a Max. He was confronted with a first-degree murder conviction for killing another man, many years in prison, and the ugly truth that his false sense of security in money had been shattered.

Shortly after his sentencing, I arrived in Seg and was able to secure a small room to meet him in. He was lost. His entire life was falling apart. Numerous times Jesse expressed the feeling that everything was hopeless. It was at this point I shared my story of conversion with him.

It wasn't very often I shared this story with men in prison. Though it might seem a missed opportunity, I've learned most men don't care much about a chaplain's personal story. What is far more important to them is if you are a "real" chaplain, someone who cares about them.

Jesse was shocked to find a lifer sitting across from him, sharing the gospel message, and finally, praying with him. Little did I know the impact that conversation would have, until that night two years later when he showed up in Chapel.

Over the next few years, Jesse and I formed a solid friendship. As this went on, I transitioned from prison chaplaincy to my work supervising chaplains for KPCI, then my position with Open Circle. Despite this, I made a point of staying in touch with Jesse.

We had many conversations, but one of them remains to me the most moving one I have ever had with an inmate—a conversation that helped me understand with clarity a gnawing theological issue I had kept quietly tucked away.

Our meeting place that day was the visiting area at Stony Mountain Institution. As we sat down, I could see there was something really bothering Jesse. "Hank, I'm getting a lot of pressure from people in a Chapel group that I am in. They keep telling me I need to forgive myself for what I have done. What do you think?"

It was my turn to be taken aback. I had closed the door to conversation around this issue a long time ago for reasons that will be obvious in a moment.

"Well," I said, "I have never forgiven myself for what I did."

There was a long pause as he looked at me in surprise. I went on to say, "I have always found self-forgiveness a bizarre concept for a Christian to buy into, that you have to forgive yourself in order to move on. I have reasons for that view which I have spent a great deal of time thinking through, but most people aren't interested in hearing them."

Jesse sat there for a moment, pain beginning to cross his face. He then uttered a sentence I will never forget. "If I forgive myself, I might get arrogant and end up being the same person I was before, doing the same things I did before."

There are places you definitely don't want to reveal too much emotion. Sitting with Jesse, in an open visiting area, was one of them. It took great strength to hold back the tide of rising emotion. Quietly, I said, "You get it. You understand."

We continued our conversation as I explained to Jesse that from my perspective, self-forgiveness was just a form of cheap grace.

My sudden swell of emotion sprang from two places. First, in the years Jesse spent inside, his life had been transformed. He is as solid a Christian as you will find behind a prison wall, a man of great integrity. The struggle he came with was real. He was confused and wanted to do the right thing. His conscience was resisting a self-forgiveness script. He wasn't sure if he was right. Second, this was the first time in many years I had the opportunity to talk with someone—who was also walking the hidden journey—and talk about a subject that had troubled me for some time.

This conversation with Jesse stands in stark contrast to another, a few years earlier, I have also not forgotten. I was called down to Seg to meet with a lifer who had just been suspended. He had spent over two decades in prison for murder, was released, and a few months later found himself back in prison due to a breach of his conditions.

His anger was evident as I bent down at his cell door to talk with him through the food slot. Bitterness poured out as he talked about being sent back. Then, loudly, he said, "I don't get it! I have forgiven myself for what I did! Why can't other people?"

I listened for a few more minutes as he lambasted the rest of the world for not forgiving him and making him end up back in prison. I said my goodbyes, promised to see him again, and walked off the range.

One of the Officers looked at me. "Well, did you give him what he wanted?"

I paused for a moment to ponder that question. "No,

actually, I didn't. He wanted the world's forgiveness. I haven't even forgiven myself for what I did, so I wasn't much help to him."

This concept of self-forgiveness has been bouncing around all kinds of groups for years. I first heard it while taking part in an encounter group in Springhill Institution. Since then, I have heard it numerous times. On occasion, I would raise my objections to the concept only to have well-meaning individuals tell me I simply didn't understand the purpose of it. I found those moments particularly offensive considering the road of faith I have travelled.

So, I'd decided to remain silent on the issue. Jesse's words of great wisdom and my encounter in segregation with a man who believed he was owed forgiveness proved to be the prodding I needed to explore this concept in writing.

To begin with, how does a person forgive themselves? Do you split yourself into two personalities, with one offering the other forgiveness?

Forgiveness is not a singular action. It involves two entities and by its very nature impacts both parties. It is in the nature of forgiveness that one is the offender and the other has been offended against. Is there an offender and one who has been offended within each of us? Am I a person who so callously took part in a robbery and murder, and at the same time another person separate from that self, and therefore because of this able to forgive myself?

This type of thinking raises an impediment in travelling the hidden journey and does not assist in the change process. If I can conveniently divorce the actions of my dark side from who I am today, there is a danger of not taking full responsibility for my actions.

Through all the years of studying Scripture I have never found a single reference to our Lord instructing us to forgive ourselves for our sinful actions. There is no hint anywhere in Scripture.

When viewed through the light of God's word, there is an air of arrogance to the concept of self-forgiveness which reverberates all the way back to the Garden of Eden. There, Satan tempts Eve with the line that God doesn't want them to eat from the fruit of the tree because "you will be like God" (Genesis 3:5). Is not the idea that we can forgive ourselves for horrible acts a bit like playing God? I need only return to the lifer in Seg to affirm this point.

The most troubling problem with self-forgiveness in a prison setting, though, is what it leads us to think about the victims of our crimes.

Let's move this conversation into a real-world scenario. I was asked to attend a parole hearing with a man I had walked the Emmaus Road with. At one point in the hearing a Parole Board member asked, "So, what do you think about your victims?"

There was silence. I watched a man I had journeyed with for a number of years drop his head, grappling to hold back powerful emotions. His eyes became moist. His entire face, which to that point had been calm, almost stoic, transformed into twisted pain.

In a soft shaky voice, he said, "If I were my victims, I wouldn't want to let me out of jail."

This time it was the Parole Board's turn to be silent. I don't believe it was the answer they expected.

He understood. The pain he had caused others was something he lived with, wrestled with, owned. He wasn't at a Parole Board hearing to present excuses for his actions, or to talk his way out of jail. Instead, he came looking for mercy and grace.

Two hours later, grace was extended to him. He was granted parole.

This individual was serving time for a very violent offence that left deep scars in numerous lives. Let's imagine his scenario from a different perspective. Instead of answering the question the way he did, let's imagine this response: "Well, I have learned to forgive myself for what I have done, so I am sure I can move on and do well on release."

How well do you think that would have gone over at a Parole Board hearing?

Having sat with numerous men at hearings and witnessing every manner of deflection, minimization, and denial, I can tell you it would not have gone well. I cringe at the thought of standing before the family and community of my victim and declaring, "Don't worry, I have forgiven myself. You can forgive me now."

There is within this perspective of forgiving oneself something so utterly disrespectful and dismissive of victims. It is completely contrary to what Scripture teaches. There we find a God who hears the cries of victims' voices calling for justice (Genesis 4).

There could be more ink spilled on this discussion, but instead let me summarize it this way. Theology matters. Not just to you as a chaplain in terms of your calling and life, but especially to those you minister with. It mattered to the two men on the road to Emmaus. It matters to men in prison trying to untangle the sometimes-perplexing intersections of psychology, philosophy, pop culture, and theology.

Difficult theological questions are part of prison chaplaincy. Working through these questions requires a willingness to wrestle with them in the context of the environment in which they are being explored.

Self-forgiveness is most definitely not a concept compatible with this call to reveal correct theology. While it might be useful in self-help groups, private counselling, or mentorship programs, in a Christian prison context, it provides the opportunity to dress oneself in cheap grace and avoid confronting Mr. Hyde.

"Then their eyes were opened and they recognized him" (v. 31)

Reg came charging into the Chapel one day just as I was walking from my office to the sanctuary. Anger and frustration oozed from his body as he stood there breathing heavily, muscles tense, a dark, almost menacing expression drifting over his face. "Hank, I'm sorry I haven't been around much. Me and the man upstairs are not getting along right now. I'm just pissed at life and Him."

"Do you want to stay and talk for a bit? I can call the Unit to let them know you're here."

"No, not right now. I'm just not ready to talk. I just wanted to let you know I am a bit off these days. I'll talk some other time."

With that he was gone. I was left standing in the vestry area of the Chapel, my heart aching for him. Reg wrestled with drugs, life, and gangs. He wanted out, but just could not find the path. We had talked often, then he drifted away.

I left the institution that day pondering our encounter, wondering what was going on in his life. Two days later, I walked back into the institution to learn that Reg had overdosed.

Not long after, I was asked to speak at his funeral. That was hard, even for someone who is used to death.

I had the opportunity to spend some time with his mother as we talked through the problems her son left this world dealing with. There was enough pain to go around for everyone.

How often I have met men in dire circumstances. A man muscled on his range, slowly losing everything he owns. Another forced into sexual slavery by the Terror who ruled the range, his eyes growing gaunter each time he showed up in Chapel. A sex offender jumped just outside the Chapel door, beaten severely, and then unable to attend the one place he felt some shelter. I could recount many more.

In the midst of all this, watching the destructive claws of a prison culture and environment strip men of dignity, self-respect, and any sense of security, a chaplain stands for the most part powerless, unable to do very much. It can easily kindle a helpless rage that can fly off in the wrong directions.

Prison ministry is not easy work. You can invest a great deal of time, energy, and personal sacrifice, only to see minimal returns. Ultimately, I have found only one counter to all of this. It comes from something I recall written on a banner that used to hang in the Chapel at Springhill Institution:

"Invoked or not, God is present."

This echoes another important aspect of the Emmaus Road story: dramatic irony. From the beginning of the story, the reader is aware of something the two men are not. Cleopas and his companion are blind to who Jesus really is. While we read the story with eyes wide open, the two companions conduct their walk, unable to see, until the moment our Lord breaks bread with them.

As one who has personally faced life and death situations, I can assure you this principle is at work in the brutal world of prison. God is present and working, sometimes even in ways that bring the Old Testament to life, as can be seen in the following story.

Mark was an ideal target. He was young, and it was his first time in prison. He was rediscovering his faith and trying hard to live it out. The problem was, he didn't have good social skills. I never determined if he had an intellectual disability. Whatever the case, he could easily be taken advantage of. One particular bully, who lived on the same range, took great delight in making his life miserable.

Mark came to see me one day. "I don't understand. I have never done anything to this guy. Why does he make my life so bad?"

The bully would go into his cell unannounced, demanding a favour or taking something of his. On the range, he constantly mocked Mark, occasionally hitting him just for sport. Pretty soon Mark found himself isolated. No one would talk with him. It became so bad Mark was afraid to step out of his cell. The bully had done his work well. Chapel became one of the only places Mark could relax for a short time. The irony in all this was that the bully would show up in Chapel once in a while. He was a big man and played the game well. He dressed in a saintly garb when he spoke with me, or talked with volunteers, but instantly shed the innocent veneer the moment he left the Chapel.

One afternoon, a very excited Mark arrived at the Chapel with news. The bully had been released. Two days later, he met a bigger bully and was shot to death in Winnipeg. I warned Mark that gloating over someone's death was not an appropriate response. Although he agreed, he was deeply thankful the bully would not be back.

His freedom was short lived. Bullies leave vacuums that other bullies jump into. Quickly, Mark found himself the target again. It was depressing to watch. Mark continued to attend Chapel, trying to live out his faith, occasionally showing up with a bruise or two.

A few months later, Mark's mood improved dramatically. He was more upbeat and engaged with people. After a service I pulled him aside and asked what was up. He smiled. The new bully had run afoul of his fellow gang members. They jumped him and beat him so severely he was now paralyzed from the waist down. He wouldn't be back on the range again.

Mark's story is not the only one where I have witnessed a strange intervention in the life of a man trying to live for Jesus Christ. Despite seeming inappropriately smug, Mark nonetheless saw God's hand at work, and I, walking alongside him, couldn't help but see it as well.

Walking alongside other inmates means, as chaplains are invited to prison ministry, we walk in as much uncertainty as Cleopas and his companion. Understanding this position of invitation has the potential to transform the way a person interacts with the group they are ministering with. There is an openness to learning, understanding what the Gospel looks like inside a prison. It orientates the chaplain as a student, willing to learn from inmate and staff alike.

Over the years, I have met numerous well-meaning individuals who firmly believed they were bringing God's Light into a dark prison. They were not bringing it in. God was already there! I knew that. I lived it.

I had come to appreciate this early on from something Charlie Taylor had shared with me, when I was still an inmate at Springhill Institution.

He had been leading a Kairos Marathon Encounter Group in the Chapel. These group sessions would take place over a two-day period.[27] The first day had been particularly draining, with one individual in crisis weighing heavily on Charlie's heart. The next morning, as Charlie travelled from the entrance of the institution down to the Chapel, the fatigue of continually coming back, along with the burden of trying to make a difference, began to overwhelm him. It felt dark, almost hopeless. Somewhere on his way down the long breezeway, as he approached the last barrier before the Chapel, he discovered Jesus walking alongside of him.

Charlie grew still as he recounted what happened next. "As I walked along, I realized that God was already here before I even arrived. I was just being invited to join him in a work He was

---

[27] The Marathons continue to be held at Springhill Institution and are organized by Concilio Prison Ministry: http://concilioprisonministry.org/

already doing. Before I came, He was here. After I left, He would be here."

There are moments in your relationship with people that prove pivotal. That was one in my relationship with Charlie. It was the first time I had encountered someone who acknowledged and lived out the reality that God was already in prison. To hear someone say they were "invited" to join a ministry that was already going on was deeply moving.

Inmates and chaplains both are God's messengers inside. Inmates are not looking for someone to bring the Gospel in. They are looking for someone to join in the work of the Gospel, to assist, teach, listen, be willing to learn from them, as they are willing to learn from us.

Invoked or Not

Phil was a transfer in from the United States and had the opportunity to finish his sentence in Canada. He was a Canadian citizen who ran afoul of the law at a young age and spent over twenty years in the American prison system. He was not the kind of man to mess with. Tough, hardened by years in two of America's toughest prisons, he could take care of himself. He was also a deeply committed Christian.

It was during a transfer to another institution that Phil ran into trouble with a fellow inmate. The insults turned into threats. Threats turned into a confrontation where Phil slit the man's throat. The man survived, and later apologized for starting the altercation.

A few days later, the man was transferred. Phil's response to the incident has stuck with me. As he recounted the incident, he said in a very humble voice, "You know, I didn't have to hurt him. God had already taken care of the problem by getting him transferred. I feel bad that I didn't trust God to take care of that situation. It taught me an important lesson about trusting God."

Most times, a chaplain is merely a channel through which help can be provided. You are faced with the harsh reality there is nothing you can do except pray and walk in the dust of the road with the one who is suffering, remembering that "Invoked or not, God is present."

"He disappeared from their sight" (v. 31)

Scripture informs us that in Jesus' day, the village of Emmaus was about eleven kilometres from Jerusalem. Assuming Jesus joined Cleopas and his friend near the beginning of their journey, and they travelled at a slow leisurely pace, it would have taken them about two and half hours to reach Emmaus. There is no indication they stopped until they reached a home in the town.

Though He agreed to stay with them, it was short-lived. The moment He broke bread in their home and they recognized Him, he vanished. Those two and a half hours together were all they got.

This seemingly inconsequential detail of the story has proven to be one of the more profound insights in my work as a chaplain. It has challenged me to always be open and sensitive to the moments you have with an individual. Your contact with them may be fleeting, yet immensely important for them and on occasion for you also, as the next two stories reveal.

A Compassionate God?

We had just finished a Chapel service and were in the process of bringing the coffee out for our fellowship time. I unlocked my office door, stepped inside, and sat down to take a short break.

As I sat back in my chair, an inmate I had never met before appeared at the door. There was no introduction, no small talk. Leaning up against the door jamb, eyeing me over, he said, "So, I don't believe in a compassionate God."

There are those moments when you know you are being baited. "So," I asked, "why not?"

"Well, I tortured my victim for fourteen hours. I can't believe that a God who claims to be compassionate can send people to be tortured for eternity."

I knew this was not the time for an eloquent discourse on the existence of hell and God's compassion. This was about far more than whether or not a compassionate God existed.

I looked at him, pondering his statement. "Would you like to sit down and talk about it for a few minutes?"

He was taken aback. This wasn't the response he expected.

Slowly, he entered the office and sat in the chair across from me. "So, what do you think of that?"

"Well," I said, "you make an interesting point. However, my belief in a heaven or a hell does not rest on any one person's particular view. As a Christian, I accept that Scripture teaches that they exist. Jesus was very clear on that point."

What followed was a twenty-minute conversation, one in which this young man grew increasingly uncomfortable, not because I was cornering him theologically, but because the real issue he was attempting to skirt was coming into sharper focus as we spoke. He was well aware his actions had caused tremendous suffering to another human being. You would have to be a psychopath not to be impacted by the cries of your victim as you tortured them.

I have met psychopaths, served time with them, worked with

them—my accomplice was one. I know what one looks like. This young man was not one of them.

The very fact he was attempting mental gymnastics with a chaplain in a Chapel and displaying signs of distress were testament to that. His reason for challenging a chaplain on the existence of a compassionate God was because he didn't want to end up in hell. His real goal was to logically eliminate a final judgement, and it wasn't working.

Eventually, it became clear to him I was just too firm in my position. He wasn't going to gain an ally to sooth his conscience, so he got up to leave. I shook his hand and told him I was always open for more conversation.

I never saw him again. I have wondered from time to time whether or not he ever opened the door to start down the road he needed to travel, his own hidden journey.

Sometimes we have the luxury of numerous encounters with individuals over an extended time. Other times, there are only a few minutes to walk in the dust of the road speaking into someone's life.

I wasn't relying on follow-up meetings, where I might convince this struggling individual about the existence of heaven or hell or even the final judgement. His conscience was already poking at his arrogance. What I tried to do in our conversation was to point him in the right direction. Otherwise, he would be haunted for the rest of his life, burying the ghosts in more drugs, booze, and violence.

A Prayer for Healing

Not all encounters are as dark as the previous one. Some are more affirming.

If a major incident occurred in the institution and the

individual or individuals involved were hospitalized outside of the institution, it was our practice as chaplains to try and visit them, especially if we had some connection with the person.

In one such instance, I found myself the lone chaplain on duty. Bo, my Catholic counterpart, was off for a few days. There had been a stabbing the night before, with the individual receiving over fifty stab wounds.

He survived! I looked him up on our information system to determine his faith affiliation. It turned out he was Catholic. Though Bo had more contact with him than me, I was the only chaplain on duty.

I checked in with the Correctional Officers at the entrance to the inmate's hospital room. As I entered, I was shocked to see a large family presence there with about fifteen people in the room.

My anxiety started to rise. You never know what you are going to encounter. After all, I was a Protestant Chaplain. Despite having small square bandages all over his body, the inmate was awake and greeted me with a warm handshake.[28] He introduced me to everyone in the room: his mother, sisters, brothers, their spouses and their children. It was quite the gathering.

We talked for a few minutes about how he was doing. I then asked, "Would you like to have a word of prayer for healing?"

"Sure, I would appreciate that."

Fifteen people, all strangers to me, bowed their heads as I prayed for a speedy recovery and the inmate's safety when he was returned to prison. I ended my prayer, and a number of those

---

[28] There are many different types of weapons used in prison stabbings, from blades to thin round rods. In this case, thin round rods attached to handles were the preferred weapons. They are easier to make, conceal, and take less force to penetrate a body.

present made the sign of the cross. I said my goodbyes and slipped out of the room.

As I stepped into the hallway, the inmate's mother caught up with me. She thanked me over and over again for taking the time to come and pray with her son and the family. It didn't matter to her what my faith tradition was. She was just thankful I was there. I assured her I would continue to pray for him.

The stabbing victim and I did not connect again for some time. Circumstances did not make it possible. Years later, as I was visiting with a few men at the minimum section of the prison, there he was. He came over.

"Hank, I wanted to let you know how much we appreciated you coming to see me that day in the hospital, especially my mom. We won't forget that."

There are numerous instances where a chaplain's connections and encounters with individuals are short, just like Jesus' encounter with the men on the road to Emmaus. Taken in the context of an entire lifetime, Jesus' short walk with these men was a fragment of time. But what an impact it had on them. They were never the same.

"Were not our hearts burning within us while he talked with us on the road?" (Luke 24:32b)

"They got up and returned at once to Jerusalem" (v. 33)

An image forms in my mind when I read the closing words of the Emmaus story. Cleopas and his friend are returning to Jerusalem, travelling the same dusty road they had walked in despair and hopelessness, up and down the same hills, around the same corners. Now they are filled with joy and excitement. Jesus appeared to them, walked with them, instructed them, revealed himself, and then left them to continue their faith journey.

This is an important lesson for those of us called to minister. It is especially relevant in a prison environment. Let me enlist the help of the Apostle Paul to expand this point. In his letter to the Philippians Paul writes: "Therefore, my dear friends, as you have always obeyed—not only in my presence, but now much more in my absence—*continue to work out your salvation with fear and trembling.*" (Philippians 2:12)

"Paul was Jewish!"

Daniel was Jewish. When he entered prison, he had little use for Christians. As his sentence drudged on, however, he found himself drawn to the fellowship in the Chapel. He had no intentions of converting—that would be the height of apostasy.

I met him in the minimum, where he would show up for groups and the occasional Chapel service. His quick wit and humour were infectious. Full of energy, Daniel was more than willing to jump into a religious debate and challenge the Christians to a contest of wit.

At least, that is what appeared on the outside. In my office, he was a different man, someone who was searching for purpose and meaning in life. We had numerous conversations about faith, life, and what his future would hold. Rarely did I bring up the subject of Christianity. I didn't have to. He knew my past, and heard my Chapel messages and views in groups.

Arriving for work one afternoon, I checked in at the Duty Desk and began the walk over to the Chapel.

One of the men approached me. "Hey, Hank, you might want to call Daniel down. He has been at the Chapel at least three times today looking for you. He seems excited."

"Okay." I wasn't sure what might be up. I didn't have long to wait. Just as I entered the office and began removing my coat, there he was at the door, almost bouncing off the ground, panting from the run over to the Chapel.

"Hey, Daniel, what's up?" I asked.

"Paul was Jewish! He was Jewish!"

Now, I was used to Daniel being a bit hyper, but this was strange. I smiled to myself, sure I was going to hear an interesting story. "Have a seat. Tell me what's going on."

"Hank, Paul was Jewish!"

"Okay, but so was Jesus."

"No, you don't understand. Paul was a Jew who converted to Christianity!"

Suddenly I caught on. This was significant for Daniel.

He continued, "I was reading a part of the New Testament and it hit me, Paul was Jewish! What the heck was my problem with the Christian faith? So I gave my life to Jesus Christ!"

Over the next few months, we spent hours working through what that meant for his life. At one point, we began talking about which church Daniel should attend. This is a question that has surfaced on a few occasions as individuals look toward release.

I did what I have done in numerous instances when asked that question. I pulled out the Apostles Creed.

"This, Daniel, is the core," I told him. "These are the basics. Everything else is minor. No denomination has the market cornered on the whole truth. Whether you are physically dunked, sprinkled or not for baptism, whether you believe in saints or not, whether non-violence is your stand in life—these and other matters, ordinances, and beliefs do not determine your Christianity. Where you are going to attend, which denomination you choose to affiliate with—these are decisions that you and God can work out."

Equipped with this, Daniel decided which church to attend.

In fact, a few months after his release, I had the opportunity to attend his baptism.

Agency

Daniel's story speaks to an important principle of good chaplaincy: empowering the agency of men who come for guidance. Some chaplains have a strong desire to engage in proselytizing for their particular brand of faith.

As a former inmate, I have a unique perspective on this. When chaplains flaunt their brand, a paternalistic attitude surfaces. It implies grown intelligent men in prison are not capable of making decisions about where they are going to anchor their faith life.

When a chaplain engages in promoting their brand, it can easily veer off into suggesting, implying, or even putting down another faith tradition. The reason, of course, is because they believe their particular brand is better.

Most men in prison who hear a chaplain putting down another faith tradition are not impressed. It can undermine the credibility of a chaplain who is called to minister to all faiths. Our calling is not to herd converts to a particular brand. Chaplains should provide a space where individuals can find help working out their salvation in fear and trembling, a space that empowers individuals to make choices about what direction they feel the Spirit of the Lord leading them. This principle of empowering agency applies to any number of areas in the lives of men in prison who come to see a chaplain.

The following incident occurred while I was an inmate working in the Chapel at Springhill.

One of our regular Chapel attenders was serving time for a

sexual offence. He spent time counselling with one of the chaplains.

One evening, he was severely beaten by a number of men. As a result, he spent a few days in hospital.

The day after the beating, the chaplain arrived at the Chapel, where I and the other lifer who worked there were doing our regular cleaning.

He was furious. "You two are his Christian brothers in the faith. You should have protected him!"

Neither I nor the other lifer said anything. We talked after the chaplain was gone. Two things became clear. First, the chaplain had no idea how prison functions—or he chose to ignore it—even though he had worked in a prison for a few years. Asking someone to stand up for a sex offender is like asking them to paint a target on their head.

Second, he had no idea what he was asking. The fact that both the other lifer and I were doing a life sentence and would lose everything if we engaged in a physical altercation, these things meant nothing to him. Protecting a favourite of his was far more important. We were expendable. Any trust I had for him left that day.

He never apologized for his outburst or his accusation that we were partially at fault for the beating. In fact, after the inmate was released back into population, the chaplain tried to prod us into providing protection for this individual by again suggesting we had some responsibility toward him.

Prison chaplaincy should be a place where someone will walk alongside of another as a spiritual friend, in the dust of the road. It is not a place where anyone gets to dictate what another should do in their walk with God. Chaplaincy should offer a space where each person can be empowered to continue the journey on their own, respecting the decisions they make – the agency God gives all of us to work out our salvation in "fear and trembling", even in the darkest of circumstances.

7. Anatomy of a Riot

A violent man entices his neighbor
and leads him down a path that is not good.
(Proverbs16:29)

Riots, disturbances, incidents—sooner or later, chaplains will find themselves in an institution where one or more of these occur. Whether it be a murder, suicide, gang fight, full scale riot, or staff assault, the routine of the institution can be upended for days, weeks, and in rare cases, months. Depending on the severity of the incident, it can impact a few inmates and staff, or encompass an entire institution.

Every incident has repercussions. Inmates can lose a close friend, be transferred to a higher security level, face more charges, endure physical injury, or struggle with trauma. Staff can be injured, as they are often the first on the scene at assaults and murders. They can endure harassment, or wrestle with debilitating trauma.[29]

The aftermath of these events can be difficult to navigate. What is the role of a prison chaplain in the aftermath of an incident? Exploring this question is critical to understanding prison chaplaincy, as it takes us deeper, to a more intricate layer of prison life where rawer emotions are laid bare, and it is impossible to share my own journey as both a lifer and a prison

---

[29] Recent research indicates that 36% of officers suffer with post-traumatic disorder: https://www.cbc.ca/news/canada/manitoba/stony-mountain-james-bloomfield-workers-compensation-corrections-canada-1.5110580

chaplain, without taking you into the heart of the most difficult incident of all: a riot.

The Setting

Elements that make up a riot can be difficult to explain to those who have never set foot in a prison. This is especially true when the structure of the institution and population dynamics play a role in how a riot develops.

One riot I was involved in occurred at Atlantic Institution in 2000. At the time, Atlantic Institution had three main units.[30] Each could house approximately eighty inmates. Unit 1 housed General Population (GP), Unit 2 was termed Protective Custody (PC), and Unit 3 was Segregation (Seg).

Each unit consisted of four ranges, two upper ranges and two lower ranges. A Control Post on the unit was staffed by a Correctional Officer at all times. All the cell doors and gates on the unit were operated from the Control Post.

On every unit, the design of each range was the same. As you entered, there would be a Common Area where inmates gathered to sit, play cards, watch TV, or prepare small meals. Beyond the Common Area were the cells of the range.

The Common Area had a TV room that could accommodate about ten people. It was enclosed by steel pillars with reinforced glass walls, entered by a door.

The reason for this design was twofold. First, it provided a space for inmates to watch TV without bothering others. Second,

---

[30] The institution now consists of two sections. The older section is called "direct observation cell ranges" and the new section is called "reduced movement out of unit". In 2000 only the first section existed.

the glass walls gave the officer in the Control Post a view into the room.

Each range was independent of any other range on the Unit. There was no movement between ranges. When inmates were released from their cells, they could only move into the Common Area on their specific range. Any movement off the range was controlled by the officer in the Control Post via a set of gates.

Of specific importance, in what will soon follow, was the population make-up on Unit 2. Three of its four ranges were PC. They housed individuals who were unable to integrate into GP. Reasons for this varied from type of offence, being labelled as an informant, or incompatibilities with individuals in GP. Incompatibility issues could be anything from gang affiliations to unresolved conflicts.

The fourth range on Unit 2 was designated Super Protective Custody (Super PC). This range was for individuals who could not live in the PC population. There were seventeen men in the Super PC population with a number of them doing time for what are considered the most horrific of crimes: murdering a child, repeated offences against children, or persistent violent sexual offences.

Relationships among the different populations can be viewed from a hierarchy perspective. GP sat at the top. Below them were the PCs. Further down the ladder were the Super PCs.

In a maximum-security prison, these population distinctions result in a high degree of hostility among the groups. That reality was one of the catalysts for the worst riot in the history of Atlantic Institution.

Riot x 2

Tuesday January 4th, 2000

I arrived at Atlantic Institution in September of 1999. In my first week as chaplain, it was evident that serious tensions existed between frontline staff, administration, and inmates. It surfaced in minor interactions and skirmishes among all three parties. Four months later, the tension boiled over and the first major incident occurred.

Around lunch time on Tuesday, January 4, 2000, GP (Unit 1) started rioting by refusing to lock up, covering the range barriers so staff could not see what was going on, then burning and destroying everything in sight. By Wednesday morning, the riot had been suppressed and staff regained control of Unit 1. A considerable amount of damage resulted from the rampage.

GP was locked down and stayed that way for months. No one was allowed out of their cells, meals were brought to the cell doors, and there was no movement onto the Unit except by security staff. At the time, it was called the worst riot in the short history of Atlantic Institution. There was worse to come.

Sunday, January 23rd, 2000

It is difficult to describe the atmosphere after a riot. They don't dissipate when they are over. A simmering anger of unfinished business hangs in the air. There is a deep distrust that permeates every interaction. Staff are on edge. Inmates are on edge. Routines are suddenly changed. There is no regular recreation, no showers, no opportunity for phone calls and visits.

Institutions crave routine. Disruptions in routine cause more tension.

On Sunday, January 23rd, 2000, the continuing tension erupted again. This time, the PC population on Unit 2 began to act up. As the disturbance escalated, the entire unit was ordered to lock up.

The three ranges that made up PC refused. The Super PC range complied, with men locking up in their respective cells. The reason for the difference in response was because the men in Super PC were well aware their safety depended on staff controlling the action happening on the other three ranges. The PC population regularly made threats toward the Super PC population.

The two lower ranges were both PC. Inmates on one of those ranges managed to breach a steel door that linked the two ranges. Approximately thirty to forty inmates began to congregate on the lower range below the Super PC population.

A plan was hatched. The PC inmates on the lower ranges decided to set a fire directly below the Super PC range and burn them to death. Their plan was to fill the TV Room with anything that would burn. The inmates travelled throughout the lower ranges, scrounging whatever could be carried: broken radios, televisions, pillows, mattresses, prison-issue winter coats, and other clothing. Almost forty cells' worth of burnable items was stuffed into the TV Room located right under the Super PC range. Then, they lit it on fire.

It is impossible to fathom the insane thought processes that would rationalize such an action. Even though they were locked in a cage with nowhere to run, they started a huge fire.

Very soon, they discovered how idiotic their plan was. The fire roared out of control, producing heat so fierce it melted the reinforced glass in the TV room.

Inmates scattered. Some rushed to the back of the range, trapping themselves there. Others raced back through the breached door over to the other lower range. The fire continued to intensify, with barrier gates becoming so hot you couldn't touch them without burning your hand.

As if staff didn't have enough dangerous problems to deal with, an even deadlier one was forming.

A large amount of the material used to fuel the fire were winter coats and mattresses. As the filling in these items burned, it gave off a thick black toxic smoke. The smoke only had one place to go: up to the range where the Super PC inmates were locked in their cells.

The situation was spiralling out of control. Staff had three separate problems to deal with. First, the PC inmates rioting on the lower ranges were now experiencing the life-threatening effects of their actions. Staff needed to get the fire under control. Secondly, PC inmates on the other upper range had attempted to breach the door to the Super PC inmate range side. Staff had to control the action there. Thirdly, the Super PC inmates on the upper range were slowly succumbing to the thick black smoke billowing up through the range into their cells. They were trapped in their cells, toxic smoke flooding their living spaces. While all of this was unfolding, a thick smoke hampered the ability of staff to see what was going on.

Screams began erupting from the Super PC range as men locked in their cells started choking. A few were able to break the glass in their cell windows to get some air. Others were not so fortunate, their efforts only producing bloody hands. A few began sticking their heads in the cell toilet, continually flushing it, as they tried to breathe.

Inmates on this range heard the screams of men in cells next to them fall silent. Others listened as fellow inmates cried out to God, convinced they would die. In a few cells, the smoke was so thick individuals couldn't see the bright fluorescent lights above, or even their hands in front of them.

At some point, staff made the decision to take on a high-risk task. A group of Correctional Officers donned air packs[31] and went up on the Super PC range to start pulling men out their cells.

It was a difficult position to be in. The Super PC population may have been on the lower rung of the prison hierarchy ladder, but it still contained very violent, dangerous men. Added to this, there were events occurring all around, rioting on the other upper range, and a fire raging below with more inmates rioting. Through thick smoke, officers went cell to cell pulling men out one at a time.

As each door was opened, staff were never sure what they would confront—a man in the throes of panic, weapon in hand, ready to charge them, or someone who had succumbed to the smoke. A few were unconscious. As one officer said, "When I pulled him out, there was nothing but black guck coming out of his mouth. He wasn't even breathing."

Men were taken off the range and rushed to the Medical Unit where all the available oxygen was used. That included what the institution had on hand and the resources from three fire departments called in to help. By Monday morning, the riot had been quelled and the fire was extinguished.

Miracles come in many forms. That night one occurred at Atlantic Institution. Not a single person lost their life.

---

[31] After the incident I was informed by one officer that he went on to a smoke-filled range with only his uniform and an air pack. Neither he nor his fellow officers were wearing other protective gear.

Aftermath

Monday, January 24th

Arriving for work, I travelled down the corridor to where the Chapel entrance was located. Before reaching the door, I was met by two of the psychologists at the institution, Roger and Will. They began to brief me on the events that had occurred.

My gut twisted into knots. This was an inmate's worst nightmare. After talking with them, I approached one of the senior management staff and asked if it was possible to pull the men from the Super PC range out of their cells. After their recovery, they had all been moved to empty Seg cells on Unit 3.

It was a bold request coming from a chaplain. The institution was scheduled to be completely locked down for two days, which meant absolutely no movement for inmates. The senior staff's response was that after the incident Psychology had worked with the inmates and that was sufficient.

My frustration began to rise. After such an event, a short check-in conversation with Psychology was not sufficient. I believed the men would be severely traumatized. For those who have never been locked in a prison cell, it is difficult to convey how terrifying their experience would have been. Cells would have become concrete coffins as men slowly suffocated.

Craig, my chaplaincy counterpart at Atlantic, arrived a short time later. We decided to approach Roger and Will to see if there was another way to deal with the men caught up in the riot. We discovered that they too were struggling, wondering what the best way forward was to deal with the seventeen men from Super PC. Pulling all seventeen men out at the same time would be very difficult.

It was eventually decided that Psychology would try to offer

Critical Incident Stress Management (CISM) debriefing sessions for the men in groups of six or seven. Craig and I were invited to be part of the debriefings. To our knowledge, this was new ground. Debriefings had never been offered to inmates before, an issue that would come back to bite the Psychology Department... more about that later.

CISM is used in many environments where traumatic events are part of the job: those of Paramedics, Police, Rescue Crews, and Correctional Officers. The plan was to use part of the CISM process called a debriefing. These are normally done within seventy-two hours of the event. They follow a structured outline where individuals are given the opportunity to talk about their experience, how it may have affected them, and then explore healthy ways of coping. It also gives the individual leading the debriefing, who is trained in CISM, an opportunity to observe participants and determine if anyone requires further assistance. After Psychology obtained approval, we planned to start that afternoon.

All inmates from Unit 2 had been moved down to empty cells on Unit 3. The seventeen Super PC inmates were on a lower range in Unit 3, the PC inmates on the two upper ones.

Around 1:00 p.m., we began the walk down to Unit 3. Unit 1 was silent as we passed by. No one was allowed out of their cells. Scarred walls, blackened bars, and damaged fixtures were stark reminders of the earlier riot.

We stopped at Unit 2. Fire hoses snaked through the hall onto the Unit, ready to extinguish any lasting remnants of the fire. Water was everywhere, still dripping down off the upper ranges. Blackened ceilings, walls, and bars, melted windows, peeling paint, burned debris scattered throughout—all stood as testament to the destructive power of hate and rage. It was a prison unit turned into an inoperable frame of steel and concrete.

Staff were on the unit checking for further damage and

potential fire hazards. They looked haggard and worn from the battle that had taken place. The damage from the two riots would be estimated to be $750,000. In today's dollars, that would equate to over $1,000,000.

We continued on to Unit 3. When we arrived at the Super PC's lower range, the PC men above them were at it again. Locked in their cells, they were smashing cell's effects, lighting items on fire, throwing them out into the hallway through the gap at the bottom of their cell doors, flooding the range,[32] and threatening the Super PCs. It was impossible to take six men out of their cells at that point. Our only option was to walk from cell to cell talking with individuals.

My worst fears were confirmed. A number were still in shock, smelling of smoke, covered in soot, staring blankly at us. Others described panic setting in as they started choking, succumbing to the smoke, slipping into unconsciousness, and waking up in the Medical Unit. Many told us how they had cried out to God in desperation, pleading with Him to save them.

It was overwhelming, men banging on their doors, making sure we didn't miss talking to them, listening to story after story of individuals staring at death, terrified. All the while, just above us, came the repeated sharp slamming sound of multiple cell doors being kicked and punched. Along with insults and threats raining down on the men below, water from the plugged toilets spilled over the edge of the top range floor, dripping down to the lower range.

---

[32] Flooding is accomplished when an inmate plugs either the cell toilet or sink, then continuously pushes the water valve button. Water floods his cell and travels out onto the range. If the inmate is on an upper range, the water eventually begins to flow down to the range below. In this situation the action was meant to cause frustration and distress to the individuals locked in cells below.

We spent an hour on the range. Men were desperate to talk about what had happened to them, especially in relation to their faith. As one individual put it, "Last night, chaplain, you had some pretty sincere Christians in this group. I heard them." He was making reference to the men who were heard crying out to God to save them. We finally had to leave. Staff were trying to pull men out one at a time for showers and we were slowing down the process.

Craig and I returned at 3:30 p.m. with a number of items that had been requested—writing paper, pens, envelopes, Bibles, anything to read. Again, we found men wanting to talk, desperate to have someone to listen to them. Over an hour later, we left, exhausted.

Tuesday, January 25th

It was a difficult night for the men in the Super PC population. On the range above, PC inmates continued to smash and bang away, threatening to kill them. In the morning, with most of the PC inmates finally asleep, Craig, Will, and one of the other psychologists were able to take the first group of six men to the TV room on the lower range. Although the debriefing went well, the PC inmates above heard us and were awake with more threats. It was clear that Unit 3 was not a good place to conduct further debriefings.

It was suggested the next one be held in the Chapel. That afternoon, six more individuals were selected. Getting them off the range was near pandemonium. Everyone who had not been in the morning group wanted to be in the next one. Men were hollering up and down the range, "When am I going to get out? I need to talk! I am going nuts in this cell!"

To get to the Chapel, we had to pass by Unit 2. A number

of the men found this difficult. Some purposely looked away as we walked by.

Entering the Chapel, we formed a circle of chairs and were about to start debriefing. As the psychologist leading the group attempted to build some dialogue with the men, he used a number of swear words. I watched as faces all around the circle began to contort and twist.

Finally, one of the men spoke up. "Hey, this is a Chapel. You don't use that kind of language in here."

The psychologist was surprised. To his credit, he handled it well, sincerely apologizing for his words. All was forgiven and we moved on.

Two and a half hours of intense emotions, frustrations, and anger poured out as person after person relived what it was like being in a locked cube of lethal smoke. There was seething anger at the men who lit the fires, bitterness at the perceived slow response of staff, and concerns about how to mentally and emotionally survive such an event.

It is quite impressive what two hours of debriefing can do in the hands of a skilled facilitator. A much calmer group of inmates returned to their cells at the end of our session.

Wednesday, January 26th

Around 9:30 a.m., we were able to take the remaining five men down to the Chapel and begin the final debriefing. The same scene unfolded: frustration and anger at not being rescued earlier, profound anger at the men who had tried to kill them, concerns about their mental health. Again, the facilitator's skill was evident as men returned to the Unit calmer than when they left.

Later that day, a meeting was held with Psychology. A

number of things were brought up, pinpointing those most traumatized and in need of further assessment and help. We discussed different strategies for follow-up with all the men.

There was also a concern raised about how to reach the perpetrators, the PC population. Not everyone in PC was a willing participant in the riot and some may have been traumatized.

This presented a thorny problem. It would be difficult to call them down for a group session. Many would not comply simply because they needed to maintain their "image" in front of peers. The institution would open an investigation and the primary ringleaders would be singled out for potential charges or transfer to another institution. Under those circumstances, no one was going to talk in a group of fellow inmates. It was suggested the chaplains do a range walk on the rest of Unit 3 where the PC population was housed and try to determine who was in need of further intervention.

Thursday, January 27th

On Thursday afternoon Craig and I headed down to Unit 3 and walked two other ranges where the PC population was housed. We found three, with a possible fourth person, displaying symptoms of severe trauma such as shock, confusion, difficulty concentrating, and feeling disconnected. Many of the men were tense, angry, and afraid of what would happen to them. Their fears were justified. As mentioned earlier, riots always have repercussions.

Friday, January 28th

Craig met with Psychology to determine what might be the

best way to proceed from this point on. It was suggested Craig and one member of the Psychology Department meet with the remainder of the men from the PC population on an individual basis and offer help. This was done in the afternoon.

Monday, January 31st

From the one-on-one sessions on Friday, two individuals asked for a debriefing. These were completed on Monday afternoon. There was also a confidential self-referral form developed and distributed by the Psychology Department, inviting individuals who wanted further counselling to send in the form.

Returning to Normal

Over the next few weeks, Craig and I continued to see individuals on a one-on-one basis. Eventually we were able to hold weekly Chapel services for the Super PC population. This only became possible once a few of the main instigators of the riot were either transferred to another institution or moved to another part of the prison. The services were crucial, though, in that they provided another opportunity for further conversations about the men's experiences from the fire.

It took months for the institution to return to normal operations. General Population (Unit 1), which had been locked down after the first riot, remained so for five months. Unit 2 returned to service one range at a time over a period of months. More inmates were transferred to other institutions.

Talk of inmates filing lawsuits filled the air. A Correctional Service of Canada Investigation was started to determine the cause of the riot, the results of which left no one happy…but that is a discussion for the next chapter.

8. Incidents and Chaplains

*For you were once darkness, but now you are light in the Lord.
Live as children of light (for the fruit of the light consists in all
goodness, righteousness and truth)
(Ephesians 5:8-9)*

On November 13, 2001, a year and half after the two riots at Atlantic Institution, Drumheller Medium Security Institution went through a riot in which one inmate was killed and another seriously injured.

I remember receiving an email from one of the chaplains there. They were trying to discern their role in the midst of the aftermath. Unfortunately, my response was probably not that helpful. I simply encouraged them to go onto the ranges and connect with the men.

I never followed up. That email exchange has bothered me to this day. I should have had more to offer my fellow chaplains who came looking for help.

Providing some guidance for chaplains in these situations is not easy. The reality of prison incidents is that no two are the same. Even within a single institution, the chaplain will find themselves facing different factors in response to an incident.

The second riot at Atlantic was unique. The population impacted most by the second riot at Atlantic Institution was the lowest of the low in the prison hierarchy. During the riot, these inmates had come within a whisper of death's door. When we entered the range the day after the riot, person after person wanted to talk to us.

On the other hand, a completely different scenario unfolded about a year later when another serious incident occurred on Unit 1, GP. We were asked to do a range walk and see if there were any concerns or needs. Craig and I were fairly certain what we would run into. GP in a Max has a different atmosphere than a PC population. Sure enough, within ten minutes of being on the range, we were accused of trying to gather information on the incident. While the occasional person would say "hello" and engage in a general conversation, no one talked.

Having worked as a chaplain through many incidents since then,[33] I never again asked a member of the senior management team to release inmates so interventions could be provided. I have learned that every incident must be treated independently—a fact I wish I could have conveyed to my fellow chaplain at Drumheller, had I known then what I know now.

Incidents have a way of bringing the elements that make for good chaplaincy into sharper focus. The reality of responding to the aftermath of specific incidents is not so much what you do, but *who* you bring and *what* you bring to the unfolding events. These will inform a chaplain's ability to provide genuine pastoral care.

---

[33] Incidents is a catch-all phrase. Commissioner's Directive 567, Management of Incidents, speaks to any number of different scenarios that can unfold in a prison: https://www.csc-scc.gc.ca/politiques-et-lois/567-cd-eng.shtml

Understanding the Value
of a Chaplain's Voice

It was not the kind of call chaplains like to get. No one wants to notify someone that a family member has passed away.

This call arrived at the worst possible time. The institution had just gone into lockdown again. GP inmates from Unit 1 had refused to come in from exercise. Usually, this would turn into a waiting game and end shortly after it started. Not this time. Inmates refused to come in for three days. They had managed to break a hole through the concrete wall that separated them from the canteen, so food was available.

Normally, there would have been no issue in notifying an inmate of a death. Even in lockdowns, individuals are pulled out of their cell and told. In this situation, there was a complication. The person whose father had passed away was one of the ringleaders in the unfolding incident. Each day, I would come into the institution, hoping to talk with Matt, whose father had passed away, only to discover the GP inmates were still refusing to come in. Finally, on the third day, the standoff came to an end, with some not-so-gentle intervention by staff.

GP inmates were taken down to Seg (Unit 3), which became another flash point for further protests. Again, I was unable to go and meet with Matt. This lasted for another two days. Repeatedly I asked, and repeatedly I was told, it was not safe to pull someone out.

Finally, on the fifth day, I was allowed to see him. I arrived on the Unit and explained to the officers what I needed to do. Then I added, "And I have to tell him the funeral has already taken place."

The two officers looked at each other. They knew the inmate. "Do you want us in the room with you?"

I pondered this for a moment. "I think it would be best if I was alone with him. He might take it better."

I, too, knew Matt. He was not a Chapel attender, but on occasion we had talked about personal struggles in his life.

The officers and I walked into the common area and I stepped into the interview room, surrounded by plexiglass walls. I sat down and waited for Matt to be escorted to the room. He was brought in and sat opposite me.

"What's up, Hank? You wouldn't be coming to see me here unless it was bad news." Matt was young and strong, with a deep hatred for authority that oozed out through his words and actions. For some people, the experience of prison brings about change and they never return. Some it breaks. Others it distorts and twists into pain-filled vessels of rage. That was Matt.

"Matt," I began. "I am really sorry to have to tell you this, but your father passed away." Silently, he stared at me. "I also need to tell you your Dad died five days ago and the funeral has already taken place. I tried to get down to see you as soon as I could, but I just kept running into barriers."

He sat there, rage welling from within. His eyes grew dark, the muscles in his face growing tense. The officers standing just outside the door were watching his every move. Slowly Matt rose from his chair, signalling our meeting was over. I rose from my seat.

We stood for a moment facing each other as he looked me directly in the eye. "Hank, if anyone else had come to tell me this, I would have lost it on them." He left the room and was escorted back to his cell.

The voice you speak with has great power to diffuse, heal, and bring peace. Or, as we saw in earlier examples, cause damage.

There have been a few Matts over the years. Men on the verge of "losing it" who were brought back from the edge by a calm, gentle intervention. It is not the actual words that matter so much as the person who conveys them, how the words are conveyed, and why they are being conveyed. Matt understood I intended him no harm. I was trying to bring a painful message in the most respectful way possible under the circumstances. I had no power to change the events that had occurred. Matt knew that and believed me when I told him I had tried to see him earlier.

I learned about the powerful value of a chaplain's voice through a gentle, compassionate person: Sister Agnès Léger. Of all the chaplains I have met, she epitomized the capacity of a chaplain's voice to speak to a full spectrum of challenges. Agnès spoke truth in a way I have seldom heard from others—not in a loud, challenging voice, but with a quiet, holy, loving firmness. She was deeply loved by both staff and inmates at Atlantic for her grace and care of all. She left a legacy of compassionate chaplaincy.

This was the model I used when raising my concerns with senior management and then Psychology after the Atlantic riot. It was one of those rare cases, when as chaplain, I felt compelled to speak into what I believed a mistreatment or injustice regarding either inmates or staff. I was deeply concerned about the trauma the Super PC population were living with and where it could lead. So, I raised my concerns in a respectful way to those who might be able to help.

There is a scriptural precedent for this type of approach found in a passage we explored earlier, from Isaiah 42:1-3, when the Lord declares, "I will put my Spirit on him and he will bring justice to the nations. He will not shout or cry out, or raise his voice in the streets." (Verses 1b-2)

An interesting connection between justice and action is established here. The passage informs us that Jesus will bring justice, but it will not be through a loud voice crying out in the street. In a correctional setting, this is of paramount importance to understand. If a chaplain chooses not to heed this insight and insists on "raising their voice in the streets", they will either create a one-way ticket out the front gate or lose the capacity to speak to injustice and pain in the future.

Understanding the Organization

As mentioned earlier, when I arrived at Atlantic Institution, it was evident there were numerous problems among administration, front line staff, and inmates. To help move the institution back on track, staff were promised a briefing on the results of the investigation regarding the first riot.

Finally, months after the second riot, the institution was shut down for the afternoon to have that briefing. Staff were invited to a Staff Assembly in the Program area to hear the results. It was a full room by the time the Warden stepped forward to read the findings.

She made her opening remarks, giving thanks for all the hard work in pulling the institution back together. Then she gave an introduction to the investigation. Finally, she announced the major cause for the first riot—a surge in inmate flu cases prior to the riot and insufficient medication available to deal with the problem.

A split second of stunned silence was followed by audible gasps from many in the room. There were whispers of "whitewash" and looks of disbelief.

The rest of the report might as well have been thrown in the trash. Any credible hope the report would identify and bring to light some of the underlying difficulties plaguing the institution was lost in the muddle of corporate wordsmithing.

To list such a simplistic reason for the complex, multilayered reality of a disturbance was difficult to hear. Riots are anything but simple to dissect.[34] The surge in flu cases and lack of medication were only a small part of bigger problems within the institution.

Most people in that room knew it. A number left the briefing demoralized and frustrated.

I am not going to spend the next few pages detailing what I, or others, believed to be the causes of either the first or second riot. My reason for sharing the above is to underline a personal definition I would like to provide. On occasion, correctional organizations can become politically entangled bureaucracies, which, powered by their own inertia, can distort the very values they claim to uphold.

"Politically entangled bureaucracies" is another way of saying everyone in a correctional system has to answer to somebody, somewhere, sometime, all the way up to the highest political level. When the system gets big, a different set of rules emerge.

An example will help illustrate this point. One day, I received a call from a Project Officer[35] at the institution. Would I have time to meet that day? A few hours later, I found myself answering questions about a Chapel volunteer whose clearance had been revoked. Chaplains don't revoke clearances. That is the business of the Security Intelligence Department in the institution. I was aware of the situation. A couple of months earlier, I had already been interviewed by a Security Intelligence Officer regarding the volunteer.

I left the meeting puzzled. Staff were in a big rush to gather information, which usually meant the request had come from higher up. Sometime later, I learned the request for information

---

[34] A detailed treatment of this process can be found in the article "Understanding prison riots: Towards a threshold theory" by Arjen Boin and William A. R. Rattray.

[35] As the term indicates, Project Officers are assigned specific projects or tasks in an institution to oversee and complete.

had come from the Minister's Office, asking why the volunteer's clearance had been revoked.

Two things struck me. First, personal political connections and clout can impact the system dramatically. Secondly, as a contract chaplain working in an institution, I was suddenly called on to answer questions that may well have found their way on to a briefing note handed to the Minister. I was not concerned about the answers I was able to give. It was, nevertheless, a good reminder of how easily one can get tangled into the intersection of politics and bureaucracy.

This is a small example of the political entanglement that can occur. I share it to highlight the reality that even an obscure chaplain can find themselves facing this reality.

This entanglement can also have an impact on how the correctional system deals with specific events.

Here's another example. An offender, who had been involved in a high-profile crime spree of robberies, was eventually paroled. A few months later, his parole was suspended. Apparently, a former business colleague was attempting to smear him in public using social media and the press to make certain accusations. His parole was suspended while the system tried to sort out the truth.

This individual, who was never short of words, sat before the Parole Board. When asked if he knew why he was back in prison, he responded, "I'm back because I failed the Globe and Mail test."

I wish I would have been there to hear the ensuing conversation. He was released again.

The "Globe and Mail test" refers to how a particular action or decision by a specific arm of government will look in the headline news. I have been told on a couple of occasions that it is a politically incorrect term to use. I find that ironic. While it may be viewed as politically incorrect, the reality is sometimes decisions are based on the test. Just to be clear, you would have to look high and low to find someone who would acknowledge its use, but it is at work nonetheless.

Added to all this, most bureaucracies have the capacity to take on a life of their own. They can develop an inertia that is hard to describe unless you have been a part of it. This inertia, which can be pushed along by personal interests or a need to deflect responsibility, can distort the very values the institution claims to uphold regarding both inmates and staff.

Using CISM with Inmates

Two examples of this inertia have stayed with me from the riots at Atlantic Institution. The first was the Psychology Department getting reprimanded because they employed a component of CISM with inmates.

The reason offered for the rebuke was that CISM was not for inmates. I found this view troubling. I had hoped some things would have changed since I left prison as an inmate fourteen years earlier. It implied the trauma experienced by a group of inmates who had just about died, through no fault of their own, did not merit further intervention simply because they were inmates. To be fair, there has been research over the last number of years that has called into question the value of single session debriefings after traumatic events.[36] However, I am very thankful that, after the second riot, Roger and Will as psychologists saw things differently and were willing to provide some type of response.

In an interesting article, Leigh Blaney contends that

---

[36] From the article "Single Session Debriefing after Psychological Trauma: A Meta-Analysis" by A.A. van Emmerik, J.H. Kamphuis, A.M. Hulsbosch, and P.M. Emmelkamp.

although CISM may not work effectively as an intervention, it does lay the groundwork for promoting a healthy way to deal with traumatic events.[37] The process opens the opportunity for individuals to talk about the event with others, and to use the coping strategies they already employ. I would suggest this was our experience with the men in the Super PC population. The debriefing provided a starting point for continued conversations with them about the event, and helpful coping strategies.

Most inmates develop some type of coping skills to deal with traumatic events. Assisting the inmates at Atlantic to use healthy coping skills became a good part of our conversations with the men in the months that followed. Yet all of this occurred with the opposing bureaucratic inertia suggesting it was the wrong course of action.

Recognizing Staff

The second example occurred shortly after Atlantic Institution was fully functional again.

The individual who was put in charge of returning the physical institution back to operational level was honoured at a special gathering. He was a gifted coordinator, dedicated to his work, and one of the nicest individuals to work with. He managed to do the job in less time than was required, and under budget. For this accomplishment, he was publicly acknowledged and awarded, and rightly so.

There was, however, in my view, an imbalance of recognition in light of what had occurred over the course of the

---

[37] The article is called "Beyond 'knee jerk' reaction: CISM as a health promotion construct" and was published in *Irish Journal of Psychology*.

riot and afterwards. It bothered me so much that I finally decided to speak to the Warden.

When I had a chance to meet with her, I asked, "Why is it that the Correctional Service of Canada is so willing to honour an individual who saves them money, an award that was rightfully earned, but does not acknowledge the Correctional Officers who went on to Super PC range, at great risk to themselves, and saved the lives of seventeen inmates?"

The Warden at the time was one of the best I have worked under. She took the time to listen to staff.

She did listen to me, even if it wasn't as I'd hoped. I heard later that a private individual initiative took place to acknowledge those officers who went up into the smoke to save lives. But there was never any public acknowledgement of their work. Publicly honouring Correctional Officers for saving the lives of criminals—especially pedophiles and child murders—may not have played well in the news (Globe and Mail test).

I do not know why they were never honoured publicly. I just know you honour people who go above and beyond—no matter the politics, or your personal view of the people they save. Sadly, I also know, against the pull of an institution's inertia, one can only do so much.

Accept, Learn, be Faithful, and Honour

There are four insights I have found useful, to help a chaplain wade through this challenge.

First, with all its shortcomings, we must accept the reality of what exists in the institution where we do our work. Although we may impact a small part of the organization, it may continue to operate the way it has long after we are gone. Instead of causing personal anguish from believing we can be David taking on

Goliath, it is best to put our energy into more productive efforts, such as learning how to work within the confines of the organization. The story of the second riot in Atlantic and its aftermath is an excellent example of what can be accomplished when chaplaincy is willing to work with other parts of a correctional organization, and when the organization itself is open to working with chaplaincy.

Second, we must learn every part of the organization we are able to. The better a chaplain knows the characteristics, strange ways, and quirks that keep a given institution running, the better equipped we are to fulfill our calling. Good chaplains are like sponges, soaking up every opportunity to learn. It has come as a surprise to me that occasionally, I meet a chaplain who does not know anything about the Commissioner's Directives, the structure of the correctional system, or have a basic understanding of the parole process, what a detention review is, or a section 810—all of which are guaranteed to come up numerous times in their work with inmates. If a chaplain does not go out and learn, they will function from within a self-made chaplaincy silo, which does not produce effective chaplaincy.

As important as accepting and learning is, we must also be faithful in the discharge of our duties. A chaplain's job description exists for a reason. I draw this advice directly from examples in the Old Testament. Neither Joseph (Genesis 39:2, Acts 7:9-10), Daniel (Daniel 1:18-20, 6:26-28), nor Nehemiah (Nehemiah 2:1-9) were able to accomplish the things they did without working diligently within the organizational structures God placed them in. A short read back into their lives reveals each one was highly respected by the people who mattered.

Lastly, as a chaplain, I have learned we must honour the commitments expected of us, within the specific working structure we are placed in. These include proper security protocols, facilitating men of different faith traditions as they try to access the appropriate representatives, along with the many other aspects that are part of a chaplain's work.

No organization as large as Corrections, with its many competing agendas, is easy to work in. But prison chaplains are not called to easy work. Just like all Christians, we are called to "live as children of light" (Ephesians 5:8), bringing light into dark places (Matthew 5:14-16).

The Danger of "Us versus Them"

"Us versus Them" is an easy trap to get caught in. This is especially dangerous for chaplains after major incidents. I've seen it happen in conversations with inmates who put staff down and then expect you to share their view. It can happen with staff who do the same. It can happen with volunteers who want to minister in prison—but not with *those* inmates—and expect you to understand.

It can even happen in the community when you attempt to engage the church in prison ministry. One chaplain, soliciting baked goods from different churches to bring in for a Christmas event, found himself in conversation with a pastor. The chaplain mentioned there were men in prison who had come to faith. The community pastor's response: "Well, that's fine, as long as they stay there."

When I first started in chaplaincy, a term used to identify one element of a chaplain's role was "neutral"—chaplains should occupy a neutral place within the workings of a prison.

I have not found this a helpful way to view chaplaincy. Neutrality implies a passive non-engagement on either side of the "Us versus Them" divide, which, if you are truly living out your role as a Christian chaplain, is a myth. Let me explain why.

"Us versus Them" can blind us to two Christian realities. The first is found in The Apostle Paul's letter to the Romans when he writes, "For all have sinned and fall short of the glory of God." (Romans 3:23)

In pondering this passage, I have come to realize that it is an important equalizer. It does not matter who you are, how high your office, how low your station in life. In God's view, we are all sinners who fall short. We all occupy the same playing field before God, so no one—be they chaplains, staff, inmates, volunteers, or community pastors—is in a place to fit anyone into the "Us versus Them" divide.

The second reality can be found in a parable Jesus gave us about a Pharisee and a Tax Collector going up to pray at the temple. The tax collector, one of the more despised members of society during Jesus' time, approaches the temple and stands at a distance. He doesn't even look to heaven. Instead, he beats his breast, crying, "God, have mercy on me, a sinner." (Luke 18:13)

The Pharisee, who was supposed to be a deeply religious man, declares, "God, I thank you that I am not like other people—robbers, evildoers, adulterers—or even like this tax collector." (Luke 18:11)

The punch line in this parable is just as relevant today as it was when Jesus first spoke it. Our Lord declares that the despised tax collector went home justified, not the Pharisee.

Like Jesus, chaplains are called to denounce hypocrisy and recognize those who truly honour God. This means not only must we acknowledge the fallacy of fitting anyone into the "Us versus Them" divide, we are further called to speak words of truth to those on either side of it. That is not neutrality.

"Us versus Them" is a lens that runs the risk of applying simple black-and-white answers to complex, multi-layered problems. When victims are defined as only being outside the prison wall and perpetrators as behind the wall, we lose sight of many men who sit in chaplains' offices recounting horror stories of abuse, whether in residential schools, chaotic home environments, or on the streets. When we look at correctional staff as insensitive, uncaring pawns of the state, we lose sight of their inherent humanity and the hard work many do while carrying their own burdens in a system that has flaws.

Chaplains are called to affirm the humanity of all against a tendency to obscure another's humanity, no matter how uncomfortable that may be for some.

Ron's Story

It was the last CISM debriefing for the Super PC. As the meeting came to a close, men were milling around the Chapel, talking with the psychologists, as they waited to be escorted back to Unit 3.

Ron spotted me off in a corner, stacking chairs. With great excitement, he explained that for some time now a lady in Scotland was corresponding with him. It took two to three weeks for letters to move back and forth between them. Two days after the second riot and fire, he received a card from her. This is what it said:

> Do not be afraid, for I have redeemed you.
> I have called you by your name;
> you are mine.
> When you walk through the waters,
> I'll be with you;
> you will never sink beneath the waves.
> When the fire is burning all around you,
> you will never be consumed by the flames.

When the fear of loneliness is looming,
then remember I am at your side.
When you dwell in the exile of the stranger,
remember you are precious in my eyes.
You are mine, O my child,
I am your Father,
and I love you with a perfect love.
(Based on Isaiah 43:1-5)[38]

As thought-provoking as this experience may have been—the letter was mailed before the riot—there is another layer to reveal.

Ron was a pedophile. This was his third time in prison. By this point in his life, his entire face was tattooed. An officer once commented to me, "I know why he tattooed his whole face. It is his way of warning people." I didn't think he was far off. Ron struggled profoundly with his sexual addiction to children.

I shared the story of Ron's poem with the late Randy Fawkes, a former chaplain at Atlantic Institution. His comment has stuck with me. "Those are the times God taps you on the shoulder and reminds you he is present, even in the darkest of places and in the darkest of lives."

The world may not look at Ron as much of a human being, but evidently God does. When we refuse to live on either side of the "Us versus Them" divide and instead speak to both, it provides God with an opportunity to use us in ways we never thought possible.

---

[38] This passage is from the song "When you walk through the waters I will be with you" by Kevin Mayhew, reprinted here with permission.

An Inside Out World

I answered a phone call from Unit 3 as I sat in my office at Atlantic Institution. Someone wanted to see a chaplain. I pulled myself out of my chair, unlocked the door to the Chapel, locked it again, and started my walk through numerous barrier gates as I made my way to Unit 3.

I arrived on the Unit to find staff dealing with a minor annoyance. "Hang on for a bit," one of them told me. "Got a guy up on B who is refusing to lock up."

I sat down to watch the action from the sidelines.

An inmate was hurling obscenities and threats at the three staff who were facing him through the range barrier. On either side of Harry, a seasoned officer, stood two junior Correctional Officers, fidgeting, unsure of what to do. The younger officers were frustrated, growing angrier by the moment at being threatened. They wanted a piece of this guy. Harry, on the other hand, quietly began talking, negotiating. He had been through a lot in his career. He knew physical handling was best left as a last resort.

It took some time, but eventually the inmate agreed to lock up and was escorted to his cell. The officers moved down to the lower range to get the man I wanted to see.

I'm not sure what I was expecting. He was a large, solidly built individual who appeared quite capable of taking care of himself in a Max. In the back of my mind I wondered, *Why are you in a Seg unit? You don't look like you need protection.*

He had arrived a few days earlier. We talked for almost an hour as he explained he was doing time for killing someone. Right now, his faith was pretty important. As I listened to the confused thoughts, fears, and worries tumbling out, I was transported back in time to 1977, when I sat in a chaplain's office in Prince Albert Penitentiary. I remember vividly all the turmoil of first finding myself in a maximum-security prison, wondering what lay around the next corner, trying desperately to hang on to my faith, and longing to make contact with someone who seemed to care.

As we sat facing each other, he talked openly about his life, how everything had gone off the rails. He was trying to make sense of it all, unsure of what his future held.

We closed with a word of prayer, heads bowed in a plexiglass cage on a maximum-security Seg unit. I offered to come back and see him again, to which he readily agreed.

I walked up to the Unit Office to sign the logbook. Usually there would be a joke or two to greet me, like, "Save another soul, padre?" There was none this time. It had been a tiring day for everyone on the Unit.

I wound my way back to the Chapel. I started sliding the big Folger-Adam key into the lock on the Chapel door, then stood there for a moment, not turning the key, staring into my office through the thin slit of safety glass that was the window in my office door. Then I looked down the hallway at the staff milling around Y-Control, frisking inmates as they passed through the checkpoint.

I turned the key, opened the door, stepped in, locked it, and sat down in my office chair.

There was something else the inmate in Seg told me, something I had, until now, been unable to process. Around that detail, the whole conversation with him seemed like an experience from another world. The reality was still taking some time to grasp.

While laying out how his life had gone off the rails, the inmate revealed he was an ex-cop, starting a sentence for manslaughter. That's why he was in Seg.

But that wasn't what had shaken me to the core. A deeper realization settled in, one that took more time to comprehend.

It seemed the world had been turned inside-out during that one meeting. In a place that had a reputation for choking life from people, an ex-con chaplain, who had spent years in prison, ministered to an ex-cop who was just starting his time.

9. Respect and Honour: Staff Relations

Give to everyone what you owe them:
If you owe taxes, pay taxes; if revenue, then revenue;
if respect, then respect; if honor, then honor.
(Romans 13:7)

I stood on a cleared mountain outcrop catching my breath. The walk up the steep slope of Mount Good had been a challenge. I was thankful we weren't going to the top. It was a perfect day, not a cloud in the sky, a whispering breeze flowing through the trees. Turning to face Cowichan Lake, I soaked in the view. Light bounced off the lake, crafting a rich display of sparkling blue water. Mountains of deep green, with small brown patches of clear-cut, swooped down to the lake.

In every direction those mountains rose. It was quiet, peaceful, the perfect place for one final service. The family had chosen well.

I waited as a number of family members moved their way up the trail to the small piece of level ground on which I and a few others stood. Muscling my emotions down, I held back the tears which were close at hand. Now was not the time. I needed a strong voice to fulfill this act of respect for a friend. Everyone took a few minutes to catch their breath.

Someone called Marilyn on a cell phone. "Are you there, Mom?"

"I'm here."

"We're about to begin."

"Okay."

The hike up was too difficult for Marilyn, so she joined us by phone from her home, which lay at the foot of the mountain. I looked around to make sure everyone was here, then asked, "Are we ready?"

I wasn't sure I was. Gazing out over the beauty of God's handiwork and the domain of eagles, I took a deep breath and began:

> In that Almighty God has received the soul of our loved one now departed, we tenderly commit his body to the air and the land in the blessed hope that as he has borne the image of the earthly, so also shall he bear the image of the heavenly.

Carefully, Brian's ashes were released into the breeze stirring through the fir trees. I continued:

> Into God's keeping, we commend our loved one now departed. Into the air and the land, which is the Lord's, we commit his body, earth to earth, ashes to ashes, dust to dust; in the full assurance that as Brian has borne the image of the earthly, so also by faith, shall he bear the image of the heavenly.

There was a gentle silence as we stood there, watching Brian's ashes drift on the air, spreading out over the side of the mountain.

We commit his spirit into the care and keeping of
a just and merciful God who by reason of faith in Jesus
Christ, has already accepted our loved one into
His eternal presence.[39]

A final prayer for everyone brought the committal service to a close.

For a few minutes, no one moved as tears flowed freely. Then, slowly, a few people began the journey back down. Others lingered, captured by their own thoughts. Within me, the internal muscles that held a mountain of emotions at bay were tiring. I needed to find a place to be alone.

The last few days had been a roller coaster—flying in from Manitoba, preparing and officiating at a funeral, and now a committal service for a man I owed an immense debt to: retired Police Chief Brian Scott.

The walk down wasn't much easier than going up. Finally, I made it to the road at the base of the mountain. I walked past the house, down the road to a park nestled by the shore. Finding an old log to sit on, still in disbelief my journey of faith had brought me here, I pondered the miracle of God's great care and grace as I gazed out over the lake, eyes blurred with tears.

If Necessary, Use Words

The day before, July 13, 2010, I stood before about eighty people at St John's Anglican Church in Duncan, British Columbia,

---

39 From page 66 *A Manual for Worship and Service* by All-Canada Baptist Publications for the Canadian Baptist Federation.

leading Brian's funeral. Many had no idea who I was, or my connection with Brian. I began the message with these words:

> What is the measure of a person? How does God weigh our lives? What is it that makes our lives valuable in God's sight? These are questions that men and women have asked for centuries, questions that have been pondered by the greatest of minds, questions that all of us will ask at some point in our lives. I am neither a great philosopher nor a great theologian, but I have seen and experienced much in life. So today I want to offer you an answer to those questions by sharing with you a very personal, deep, unique friendship that began thirty-four years ago.
>
> This was a friendship that began under the strangest of circumstances, with one person on the right side of the law and the other on the wrong side. The first time I met Brian, it was in a small basement apartment in Edmonton. He was on the other end of a .38 revolver jammed into the back of my neck. His first words of greeting were not the warmest for the beginnings of a friendship. In a clear, powerful, no-nonsense voice, he declared, "Edmonton City Police. Don't move. You're under arrest."

Suffice it to say, when I was arrested there were those who were keen to take a nineteen-year-old drug addict charged with murder and grind him into the dust. On more than one occasion Brian intervened to prevent that from happening. At the time, I had no idea why he was different or what to make of his care in the darkest of circumstances. All I knew was, in the sea of people who despised my existence, he stepped in to offer a measure of compassion and act with an integrity I did not expect, especially from a police officer.

His care even extended to my family. He connected with them and offered sincere compassion to parents who were devastated by the evil their son had taken part in.

At the time, I had little appreciation or care for anything to do with law enforcement. One does not engage in a life of crime without having a low opinion of people in uniform. My encounters in the past had not been the best.

Soon, I was sentenced and went off to serve prison time. To my great surprise, Brian stayed in touch with my mom. Every year, Marilyn, Brian's wife, would send a Christmas card to her and ask about me. On a couple of occasions, while serving time, I was pulled aside by a puzzled Case Management Officer who told me Brian had called to see how I was doing.

A year and a half after my release, Linda and I planned to marry. We decided to send Brian and Marilyn an invitation. I never expected them to show up at a parolee's wedding. I just wanted to recognize his impact on my life and let him know I was doing okay. To my great surprise, a few weeks later we received a letter from Marilyn, detailing how disappointed they were at not being able to make it. Something had come up which made it impossible for them to come. I was deeply humbled; these folks were the real deal. From Christmas 1987 onward, without fail, we would receive a card and a note written by Marilyn.

Cops and cons aren't supposed to form these kinds of connections. They are frowned upon. I knew that and kept my distance. During the years after my release and while Brian was an active officer, we connected through one phone call.

Brian retired in September of 1995. He'd spent twenty-eight years with the Edmonton City Police, rising to head the Major

Crimes Unit. For the last seven years of his career, he was Police Chief in Brandon, Manitoba.

It was not until the summer of 2009, thirty-two years after he arrested me, that Brian and I would meet again in person. It was also the first time I would meet Marilyn.

There was an instant connection. The following year, Linda and I travelled to Vancouver Island for vacation. Part of our reason for going was to visit with Marilyn and Brian. After Brian's retirement, they had moved there to their mountainside home, in the town of Youbou. Unfortunately, Brian had been hospitalized and was dealing with cancer.

Linda and I spent a week on the Island. We scheduled our daily touring so we could take a portion of each day and be with them at the hospital. It was on the third day, after visiting, that Linda shared a conversation she had with Marilyn.

She waited for the right time to talk. "I spoke with Marilyn today."

"Oh, what's up?"

"Marilyn wanted me to ask if you would be willing to do Brian's funeral. She has talked with the rest of the family and they all agree."

I didn't know what to say. I was deeply humbled and conflicted. Why would the family want an ex-con like me doing the funeral? I wanted to decline, but how could I say no when I had been asked?

Filled with apprehension about what would follow, I agreed. I could not figure out why they wanted me to do the service.

A month and half later, Brian passed away.

I returned to Vancouver Island and made my way up to Youbou. I was greeted by the entire family. Even though they had never met me before, they knew me. Over the years, as I had travelled through prison, marriage, children, university, seminary, pastoral ministry, and chaplaincy I had become a shadow family member without even knowing it. From the beginning, Brian had seen something in my life I could not see. He brought home regular updates on how I was doing. Everyone wanted to know more about my life. I spent hours talking with them.

The message I delivered at Brian's funeral turned out to be the most difficult I had ever composed, not because words are hard for me to put together, but because I wanted to pay due respect to someone to whom I owed so much. I took, as my text for the message, Matthew 25:34-40. In this passage, the King separates those who will receive an eternal reward and those who will not, based on their actions in this life. Here are the closing words of my message:

> Brian was a very private man, private about a number of things in his life including his faith. Some could easily have mistaken his privacy as a sign that no faith existed. His actions revealed exactly the opposite. How does a man with no faith stay married to a beautiful wife for fifty-three years and raise five incredible children? How does a man engage in thirty-five years of police work, one of the toughest professions there is—where you are constantly encountering the darkest of human existence—and still maintain a compassion and care for others? How does a man who saw the results of countless acts of evil find the resolve and willingness to reach out to a nineteen-year-old drug addict who to most was a write off?
>
> The title of my message today is a quote that is often attributed to Saint Francis of Assisi, although no one is sure that he is the author. "Preach the Gospel always and if necessary, use

words." Somehow, I think Brian would have understood this quote because in a number of respects he lived it. When people were hungry, he gave them something to eat, when they were thirsty, he gave them something to drink, when there were strangers at his door, he invited them in, when people needed clothes, he clothed them, when they were sick, he looked after them, when I was in prison, he came to visit me.

The Challenge

On July 27, 2017, Marilyn passed away. Again, I found myself travelling to Vancouver Island to conduct a Celebration of Life service. In that message, I mentioned that one of the things I really enjoyed about finally connecting with Brian and Marilyn was watching them interact. I remarked, "Remember, this was the cop who arrested me, and here was this tiny petite woman stick-handling him like nobody's business. I thought, *So much for the tough cop image.*"

I share this little vignette to unfold the gift Brian gave me—a gift crucial to the call God placed on my life. Brian revealed the human side of law enforcement. Where I had seen hard, cold, uncaring power, he pulled the curtain back to reveal another side of authority.

To appreciate how significant this was, both in my personal life and ministry, we need to return to the aftermath of the second riot at Atlantic Institution.

It was the third day. I had spent the morning working with Psychology to bring the last group of men down to the Chapel for debriefing. We listened to more stories of choking smoke, panic, and near-death experiences. That afternoon, I met with Psychology and then made another trip down to Unit 3 to drop off some items.

Although the tension level had diminished, the range was still filled with traumatized individuals hungry to talk. I had only planned to spend a few minutes on the range. It turned into an hour and a half as I moved between cells listening.

Finally, there was no energy left. Leaving Unit 3, I began the walk back to the Chapel, passing by the burned-out hulk of Unit 2, and the silence of Unit 1 in lockdown. As I approached Y-Control, there was a group of officers gathered around talking about the events of the last few days. Passing by the group, I barely acknowledged them.

Then, just as I moved by them and started down the hallway where the Chapel door was located, something caught my ear. "You know, we should have left the bastards up there to burn." I stopped in mid-stride.

Perhaps it was the fatigue, the continuous exposure to repeated stories of near-death experiences, all wrapped up in an ex-con's journey of doing time. Suddenly, white hot rage shot through my body. My fists clenched and every muscle in my body snapped taut. Bitter anger flowed through my heart and mind. I began to turn around, planning to walk back to the group and let loose with a verbal assault. I didn't get a chance.

It is difficult to describe in words what happened. A voice spoke, as clearly as if someone were right beside me. "Hank, I have called you to be their chaplain too."

I knew the voice. It had the same firm quality as the grip that had long ago held my broken life from falling into the abyss.

My head dropped. My clenched fists released. I was stunned into silence. After a moment, I walked over to the Chapel door located a few feet away, unlocked the door, stepped into the Chapel, and locked the door behind me. I dropped into a chair in the sanctuary and sat there, staring at the crucifix hanging over the altar.

A profound reckoning had just begun in my life, one that plunged me into a period of deep soul-searching regarding my own life, God's calling, and the biases that infected my heart. Over the weeks that followed, I wrestled with the abuses of power I had witnessed in all my time involved with Corrections—the threats, intentional humiliations, hatred, and darker events burned into my memory. Of these, one of my first memories from my time inside—a memory I'd kept safely tucked away in one of those dark caverns of the past—now bounded to the surface...the inmate in the cell next to me, beaten by an officer until his pleading to stop was drowned out by another fist to the face.

I wondered, *Do I need to walk out and never return?*

Quietly, I wrestled with God. I was here in this place, answering his call. Now his voice was haunting my angry rebellious heart, with His words, "Hank, I have called you to be their chaplain too."

It is painful to have the light of God's words penetrate into the hidden angers of one's life. As I questioned, wondered, and searched, Brian surfaced in my thoughts and my heart. I began to realize God had brought Brian into my life for this point in time.

I would not have been able to carry on as a prison chaplain without Brian's impact on my life. He opened a crack in my view of those who wore a uniform. Over the next few months, God took the crack, pulled it wide open, and challenged some of my views and anger-fuelled preconceptions.

The anger dissipated. Perceptions began to change. In their place emerged a deep appreciation and understanding of the challenges staff face on a regular basis, along with the impact those challenges have on their lives and the lives of their loved ones.

Reality Check

I did not plan to start this chapter on a mountain on Vancouver Island. I would have preferred to keep that private. It was a deeply personal experience.

But as I searched for a way to address the issue of a chaplain's need to respect and care for staff, it became clear that simply stating the obvious would probably not communicate the weight I believe God gives to this important aspect of prison chaplaincy. Along with understanding the difficult challenges correctional staff face, chaplains are also called to offer the same care and concern to staff they offer to those who are imprisoned.

During my career as a prison chaplain, I have been asked to speak at a staff funeral, conduct the funeral of a young Correctional Officer who suddenly passed away because of medical complications, conduct a Celebration of Life service for a Parole Officer, and speak at a Celebration of Life service for a long-time Correctional Officer. Along with fellow chaplains and other staff, I have helped plan yearly National Day of Mourning services[40] and a memorial service for a parole officer.

One thing I have found, and instructed many chaplains in, is these services are *not* a place to either expound on great theological skills or to evangelize. They are a place to honour the life, work, and gift of another. It is imperative a chaplain work with the family, colleagues, and institutional protocols that exist to make this a central aspect of the service.

Some of the most humbling words I have ever received regarding a staff service arrived a couple of days after I officiated at the funeral of an officer. His death had been unexpected and left a tremendous hole in the life of the institution. His wife, who

---

[40] These are explained further at: https://canadianlabour.ca/day-of-mourning-2021-the-human-cost-of-covid-19/

was also a Correctional Officer, asked me to officiate at the funeral.

Here is part of the email I received from another staff member:

> Hank, just wanted to say what a wonderful job you did at the funeral on Monday. Angela made a wise choice when she asked you to do the service. No one could have done it better. Your personal touch to each member of the family was really moving. During the service, I was thinking about how well you chose your profession.

I have hung on to that email as a reminder, an affirmation about how important it is to live out this call to care for everyone.

But this capacity and willingness to offer the same care and concern to staff is about far more than just providing services. If lived out daily, it has the capacity to impact three important areas of a prison chaplain's work.

1. Once A Con, Always A Con?

There is a question I am sometimes asked. It usually comes from someone who has spent time reflecting on the awkwardness of my journey in a correctional environment. "So, how do staff react to having an ex-con chaplain in their midst?"

My best answer: "Some thought it was great, a number weren't sure what to do with it, and a few firmly believed in the old prison adage, 'Once a con, always a con.'"

The latter would have been quite happy to see me escorted out the front gate permanently. Navigating these differing positions was not always easy.

Snide remarks, lack of response to questions, or outright disrespect have surfaced on occasion in my calling as a prison chaplain. In each of these situations, I strove to live out the calling in my life to care for those around me, no matter who they were, or what power they did or did not hold. Everyone was given the same respect, even when that respect was not returned, dismissed, or mocked. In time, as staff began to recognize the values I lived by, that respect was returned in numerous ways I never expected.

I raise this part of my journey because of a complaint a few new chaplains have voiced over the years: "They don't seem to treat me or the office of the chaplain with much respect."

For new chaplains, it can come as a surprise that occasionally staff are gruff with them, or less than willing to offer a helping hand. Chaplains can assume the prison world is similar to the community where most clergy are treated with some measure of respect.

The reality inside the wall is quite different. No one hands you respect in a prison. You earn it, one day at a time, one interaction at a time, one crisis at a time. Sometimes, it takes years to build respect and rapport with staff. A few may never want anything to do with you.

You will be challenged and tested in both serious and humorous ways. Occasionally, I have wondered if the comment about "leaving the bastards up there to burn" was thrown out, within earshot, to see what kind of reaction it would solicit from me. You may be asked your opinion on divisive subjects to clarify where you stand—"Chaplain, what do you think they should do with all the clergy pedophiles?"—or, you may be challenged on your own morals and values.

During the first few months at Atlantic Institution, I had to go up to the Visiting and Correspondence area to deal with a Bible that had been mailed in. As I approached the two officers on duty in the visiting area, it was evident they were enjoying the centrefold pullout of an old Playboy magazine.

Staring at the picture intently, neither acknowledged my presence until suddenly, the one holding the magazine turned it around and pushed the centrefold view directly into my line of sight. "So, Chaplain, what do you think of that?"

I looked at the picture for a moment, then looking back at the officers said, "You know, guys, I have a wife at home that looks a heck of a lot better than that."

"Hey, Chaplain, that was a good answer!"

I realize my journey may have been a bit more intense than other chaplains, but I can assure you, even if you're not an ex-con, there is only one way to develop respect with staff. You must care about them and the world they are called to work in. You must understand and appreciate the difficulties they face. Only through showing true care and concern for staff can a chaplain build the respect and credibility necessary to do effective work in a prison setting.

This means holding your judgements, anger, and complaints in check. It means being gracious when you would rather not. It means living out your calling as "Christ's Ambassadors" (1 Corinthians 5:20) with everyone, everywhere.

2. Building a Foundation

The second area I would like to explore is so simple it is often missed. A crucial dynamic that enables a prison chaplain to function well in an institution is the working relationships they form with other staff. The foundation of those relationships is learning to appreciate and respect the important work fellow staff do.

One morning in my time working at Stony Mountain, I received a call from Emma, one of the Indigenous Liaison

Officers (ILO)[41] at the institution. "Morning, Hank. Wondering if you might be able to help me out. I need to go to Seg and meet with Randy. He just lost another family member. This will be his fifth loss since he has been in. I know you see him regularly and he gets along well with you."

"Sure. I can meet you in Seg."

Emma and I connected in Seg and asked for Randy to be pulled out of his cell. We moved into the interview room, sat down, and waited for him to be brought in. Neither of us said very much. Randy was young, too young to have lost so many close family members. This would be tough. As soon as Randy entered the room, he knew something was up.

Walking over to the empty chair he remarked, "With both of you here I know this is bad news, so just tell me straight up."

Emma gently informed him of the passing of another family member. There were a couple of moments of stony silence.

Suddenly, Randy jumped up from his seat. I have never heard such a painful scream of rage erupt from another human being. He went over to the wall and began pounding it with both fists. Howls of emotional pain reverberated around the room, through the closed door, and out into the control post area.

In seconds, three officers rushed in through the door. By this time, I was on my feet, standing a few feet away from Randy and facing the first officer. He asked, "Hank, is everything okay?"

I looked at Randy. His eyes were blazing with rage and he was already in a fighting stance, ready to try and fend off any attempt to grab him. I looked at Emma. She nodded an

---

[41] I have chosen to use the term Indigenous Liaison Officer as this is now the preferred title. The Correctional Service of Canada still lists the position as Aboriginal Liaison Officer: https://www.csc-scc.gc.ca/careers/003001-1201-eng.shtml

affirmative. "I believe we will be okay if we could have a few more minutes with him."

The lead officer took a minute to gauge the situation. Looking at both Emma and I, he said, "Okay, we will be right outside if you need us."

The officers exited the room, Randy's eyes following their every step.

It took another five minutes to coax him away from the wall and get him to sit down. We then spent the next twenty minutes talking. At the end of our conversation, he was quietly escorted back to his cell.

Earlier, I shared a passage from my friend Rod Carter's article on prison chaplaincy, *Days of Diamonds, Days of Stone.*[42] That was a day of stone.

Let's take a closer look at what happened in this incident from a working relationship perspective. First, Emma would never have called me to help break the news to Randy if we did not have a good working relationship. When you are facing this kind of disclosure, with the potential for a strong negative reaction, you need to have a certain level of trust in the person you are working with. That trust only builds over time and it only forms if you are willing to respect and appreciate the work another does.

Secondly, I was very grateful for the way the officers dealt with us. Correctional Officers don't just deal with inmate issues. Part of their role is to keep staff safe. Most take that very seriously. The officers didn't come rushing through the door only to subdue an angry inmate. They were there to keep us safe. As such, they were in charge. They could just as easily have ordered us out of the room and dealt with Randy as they saw fit, whether

---

[42] The full article can be found on pages 29-30 of *The United Church Observer,* September 1996.

that meant negotiating with him or physically handling him. Instead, they chose to let us continue to deal with him. That decision was not made lightly. It required a level of trust on the part of the officers. If, after they left the room, either Emma or I would have been injured, there would have been tough questions asked.

After Randy was escorted back to his cell, I had a chance to speak with the first officer through the door. I thanked him for allowing us to finish our conversation.

He smiled. "No problem. Just another day in Seg."

Respect. It's a valuable gift in a place where it can be in short supply.

3. Learning Curve

The third area to explore is illustrated through an experience I had in my last month at Atlantic Institution.

Staff decided to have a farewell for me. Partway through the event I was asked to say a few words. As I stood in front of about sixty staff, there were a number of things that entered my mind. However, I decided to limit my remarks to two individuals. The first was Mike, my supervisor, the Assistant Warden of Correctional Programs. I thanked him for taking a chance on me. He was part of the hiring process and took a risk. He knew it and I knew it.

Then I turned my attention to someone who never expected me to say a word about him—Bill, the Correctional Supervisor on Unit 3. As I began to talk, I could see the shock on his face. I figured, *Well, I am in over my head now. I might as well keep going.*

"Bill," I said, "of all the people I have worked with in Atlantic Institution, you taught me one of the most important lessons I could ever have learned through the way you ran Unit 3.

Day in and day out, with all the mayhem that is a part of that place, you displayed a professionalism I have never seen before. Thank you for what you showed me and taught me."

Two days later, just as I opened the door to my office, one of the officers came over. "Got a minute?"

"Sure."

We stepped into the office. "Hank, do you know what Bill is going around saying about you?"

My heart skipped a beat. I thought, *Uh-oh, what have I done?*

He continued. "Bill is walking around here and telling people you are the best fucking chaplain Atlantic Institution ever had."

Considering the author of the comment, that was a real compliment. I once thought about having those words put on a plaque to hang in my office. Just as quickly, I realized some may not appreciate it as much as I did.

Bill was a seasoned Correctional Officer…tough when he needed to be, and very committed to the staff that worked under him. Officers trusted his judgement. Below the rough exterior was a man of integrity who cared about his job and those he worked with. Bill always gave you a straight answer, using the best English vocabulary to make his point, whether it was convenient or not.

I would usually do a Seg walk once a week. Occasionally, the Unit would be in the middle of some mini-crisis. As I walked onto the Unit those days, Bill would holler above the noise, "Hank, not a good day!"

"Okay, Bill, be back tomorrow."

On two occasions I waited thirty minutes to see an inmate while a problem on a range was being dealt with. Suddenly, another staff member rushed onto the Unit, stepped in front of me, and declared they had to see a particular inmate right away.

Bill looked the staff up and down and then said, "Hank has been waiting for the last half hour. Come on, Hank."

That was Bill. For him, this lowly chaplain stood on equal ground with everyone else.

I have placed this vignette at the end of the chapter, because the final area I would like to explore concerning care and concern for staff, is the most overlooked of all. Every new first-time chaplain walking into a prison is an absolute greenhorn. The vast majority of chaplains starting work in a federal prison know nothing about how a prison works, the relationship dynamics that exist, the numerous security concerns that can arise, and the types of individuals they will be dealing with.

Nobody is going to teach you more about the correctional world than the people who reside in it and work in it. If a chaplain only listens to the descriptions and wisdom offered by inmates, their understanding of how a correctional system works will be dramatically unbalanced.

Over the years, some of my best teachers were the staff I had the privilege of interacting with. These included Wardens, Deputy and Assistant Wardens, Correctional Officers, Parole Officers, Psychologists, Security Intelligence Officers, Indigenous Elders, Liaison Officers, Kitchen Staff, Shop Instructors, Teachers, and Trades staff. There is not a single area of an institutional operation where I have not learned something from somebody.

But there is a catch. To learn, you have to be willing to observe, listen, and on occasion face a corrective reprimand.

If you don't care about staff, or show any concern for their challenges, don't expect them to be in a hurry to teach you about a world you know little about. Ultimately, one of the most important keys to being a good chaplain is to live out the Scriptural instruction:

"Give to everyone what you owe them: If you owe taxes, pay

taxes; if revenue, then revenue; *if respect, then respect; if honour, then honour.*" (Romans 13:1-7)

10. Encountering Deception and Violence

I am sending you out like sheep among wolves.
Therefore be as shrewd as snakes and as innocent as doves.
(Matthew 10:16)

A number of years ago, I designed a one-day workshop titled, *Staying Safe in Chaplaincy*. The workshop was based partially on a set of "Survival Signals" formulated in *The Gift of Fear*, by Gavin DeBecker.[43] The workshop was taught to both provincial and federal prison chaplains. I incorporated it into a prison chaplaincy course at Booth University College.

The catalyst for designing the workshop were two incidents.

The first involved a male chaplain who came very close to being sexually assaulted and murdered. His salvation can be attributed to a quick recognition of the danger he faced, and divine intervention.

The second incident did not end so well. It involved a community chaplain who was working with a recently released offender. The chaplain was lured into a vulnerable place, beaten, then forced to withdraw funds from an ATM.

The need for this type of chaplaincy training was reinforced by two interactions I had while teaching the workshop. The first occurred when I used Jesus' words to his disciples concerning

---

[43] These signals are found on pages 63-88 of the book.

their engagement with the world—"I am sending you out like sheep among wolves. Therefore be as shrewd as snakes and as innocent as doves." (Matthew 10:16)

One of the chaplains took exception to my framing inmates as wolves. Before I could respond, one of the older seasoned chaplains piped in, "If you think some of the guys coming down to your Chapel service are not going back onto their ranges and acting like wolves, you live in a fantasy world."

The second interaction occurred during another workshop while we were having a discussion about the need to wear a Personal Portable Alarm (PPA)[44]. One chaplain indicated he did not wear his alarm. I asked him why.

"Because of the message it sends."

"Well, what kind of message does it send?" I asked.

"That I don't trust them."

I looked at him directly and exclaimed, "That is exactly the message you want them to hear!"

He was dumbfounded, perhaps because the response came from an ex-con. I explained to him a PPA was not just for his protection. It was for everybody's safety. I gently pressed him, asking what he would do if an inmate fight broke out in the Chapel and the PPA was sitting on the desk in the chaplain's office? What would he do if a suicidal inmate entered the Chapel with volunteers present and began threatening to kill himself? What would he do if an inmate entered the Chapel and attempted to take him hostage?

Each of the above events has occurred with chaplains. Although they are rare, the fact that they happened tells us they

---

[44] A Personal Portable Alarm (PPA) is worn on your belt. It is standard issue in federal prisons. You are required to wear one in certain locations, such as the Chapel. It is a small device with a big red button on it. When you press the button, it signals to staff you have an emergency situation.

will happen again. Inmates who have been around for a while and value the Chapel space have no problem with the chaplain wearing a PPA. They understand who the PPA is meant for and what can happen in a Chapel.

This comes mostly from a piece of wisdom I learned from Charlie Taylor that I have used for years when training chaplains: "You cannot have good chaplaincy without good security."

Individuals attend Chapel services because it is one of the few safe places to gather. Part of a chaplain's role is to ensure the Chapel is safe by adhering to the safety protocols which are part of a prison environment.

Some chaplains, especially new ones, tend to view the prison landscape with a high degree of naivety. Shedding that naivety requires a transformation in how we see the world around us. Such a shift can rock some of our most cherished belief systems, values and perceptions.

It is difficult because as our view of the world changes, we as chaplains are called upon to continually engage others with consistent care and compassion. This can be exceedingly hard when we encounter deception or violence.

Throughout my years of serving time and working in prison chaplaincy I have witnessed numerous individuals who were unable to effectively navigate encounters with deception or violence. When this occurred, there were usually one of two outcomes.

The first would see an individual refuse to accept the reality they worked in, becoming more entrenched in their naive view. This would lead to poor judgements and dangerous actions. The second crafted a bitter, disillusioned individual who distrusted everyone.

Neither of these two outcomes provide for good chaplaincy.

Deception

Scenario 1

A chaplain will meet many different individuals attending Chapel. Some come for a short time, others longer. Then there are those who stand out. They are the ones who appear to have gone through a major change in their lives. From your limited perspective, everything points to what some would term "a true conversion".

Peter was one of those individuals. Over six years, he became a main fixture of Chapel life, rarely missing a service, Bible study, or event.

His outgoing nature soon won him attention from several volunteers. Peter was intelligent, diligent in Scriptural studies, and could hold his own in a theological discussion or challenge. He regularly brought other men to Chapel.

In time, he began to show up at my door looking for counselling and support. Our discussions slowly moved from the mundane to the more serious. In time, he admitted he was doing time for sexual offences.

Our conversations ranged from personal struggles, theology, and family, to difficulties with staff and other inmates. In all of these conversations, Peter's faith appeared to play a vital role. He would often talk about how big a difference his conversion was making in his life. He shared his faith with numerous other men, bringing them to Chapel and leading one man to Christ.

His life appeared to be truly transformed. When conversation would drift toward his criminal convictions, however, he would say something along the lines of, "I have done some horrible things in my life." In the entire six years I knew him, he never talked directly about his offences.

Peter was transferred for a year to the Regional Treatment Centre so he could attend a program for sex offenders. When he returned, I asked how things had gone. His response was everything had gone quite well; he had completed the required program. It all might have seemed fine, until I found out Peter was scheduled for a Detention Review Hearing.

Every offender, except for lifers, has a statutory-release date set at two-thirds of their sentence. At that point, they are released into the community under supervision. This supervision continues until warrant-expiry date, the date when their sentence is completed.

In cases where the Correctional Service of Canada (CSC) and the Parole Board of Canada (PBC) feel an individual is at high risk to re-offend, they can detain an offender past their statutory-release date, until their warrant-expiry date. This is done at a Detention Review Hearing. In this hearing, an offender is given the opportunity to appear before a review board consisting of Parole Board members. They are able to present any information that could dissuade the Board from enforcing a detention.

Peter asked me to be present at his hearing to offer him support. I agreed.

The day of the detention review arrived. What unfolded over the next two hours was the story of a man who, for the last twenty years of his life, had groomed victims over extended periods of time, often using the victim's caregiver as a gateway to a young girl.

Grooming is a process whereby a perpetrator plans to sexually exploit a child. They seek out vulnerable children. Over an extended period of time, they gain the trust of the child and the child's caregivers. Once the abuse begins, they use any number of techniques to maintain the child's silence. For Peter, this cycle had repeated itself numerous times.

Ultimately, the Parole Board ordered Peter be detained for his entire sentence.

Peter, of course, was upset with the decision. He never-theless indicated he was committed to moving forward. He continued to affirm his strong faith, coming to Chapel, attending all the available groups, and meeting with me on a regular basis. In time though, this storyline, along with another, would collide to create a great deal of pain in the lives of a few people.

Early in his sentence, Peter had connected with a prison visitation program and was matched with a volunteer named Ken. Ken was a deeply committed Christian. For six years, he visited Peter regularly. Ken's life revolved around family and an active church life, with a strong emphasis on living out his Christian commitment.

Over time, Ken and Peter developed a close relationship. Plans were made for Ken and his family to be a part of Peter's release. I watched this relationship grow over six years with at first interest, then later, angst.

Peter would often tell me about the conversations he had with Ken, and how important Ken was to him. Peter repeatedly said Ken was just like a brother to him, a true friend. On a couple of occasions, I asked Peter if he had ever informed Ken about what he was serving time for. He brushed the question aside, giving a non-committal answer. As Peter's release date grew closer my concern continued to grow that the friendship between Ken and himself was a potential train wreck waiting to happen.

One morning, I arrived at the institution to the news that Peter was in segregation. He had been implicated in moving contraband (drugs and tobacco) through the institution. As is often the case in these situations, truth is a rare commodity. Ultimately, how deeply Peter was involved in the smuggling enterprise will never be fully known. I, nevertheless, was fairly confident he was more involved than he was telling me.

This brought our relationship to a head, along with his relationship with Ken. I had agreed to help support Peter on his release, providing him with connections to resources, and following up with him in the community. The events that had unfolded thus far were giving me food for second thought. I was also fielding calls from Ken, wanting to know what was happening. Why was his Christian friend now in segregation? What had he done? What had happened?

This is a difficult situation for a prison chaplain to be in. Your role and position prevent you from sharing information, despite knowing that not sharing it will only create further pain.

Finally, I asked Ken if Peter had ever told him what he was serving time for. His response informed me he knew nothing about the offences. In fact, Peter had told Ken he was serving time for theft. He was deliberately presenting a false story of what he was serving time for.

Most troubling of all, was the fact that Ken had children.

I confronted Peter, telling him he owed Ken an explanation about his offences if he expected the friendship to continue into the community. As a father, he had a right to know.

In response to my prodding, Peter wrote a letter. Ken received the letter and spent some time talking with me about the contents. Despite my insistence, Peter still had not revealed the full extent of his offences.

It was only a month before Peter's release. For high-risk sex offenders, it is common for the court to impose community supervision past warrant expiry. This is called a section 810. I knew Peter would be candidate for this process.[45]

---

[45] A Section 810 refers to a section of the Criminal Code that allows the Court to impose specific conditions on a high-risk offender who has completed their sentence and is being released from either a provincial or federal prison. The individual is required to enter into a recognizance, similar to

A section 810 is accompanied by a media release, with warnings to the community that appear in every news outlet, sometimes even on the front page of the paper. This meant it would soon become public knowledge what Peter was serving time for. I didn't want Ken to find out that way.

Finally, I revealed Peter's offences to him, and what the implications of a section 810 were. Ken was confused, angry, and deeply hurt. His personal world was turned upside-down. He believed his friendship with Peter was built on truth and honesty. It wasn't. All the time and energy he had put into establishing the friendship over a six-year period was based on exactly the opposite.

My relationship with Peter had reached a point of decision. It was time to have a tough conversation.

We sat down in an interview room in segregation. Over the next half hour, I detailed my concerns and confronted his deceptions, reminding him I had attended his detention review and knew the details of his lengthy criminal offending. I challenged him on the fact that he had repeatedly lied to Ken about his offences, someone who meant him no harm, and now all his community supports were evaporating.

Some moments sear into your memory. Peter's response was one of those. A man I had spent six years working with as a chaplain, a man I had numerous in-depth personal faith conversations with, a man who claimed dramatic spiritual change in his life, looked at me and with whatever mask of sincerity he could muster, stated, "Hank, I really feel sorry for those poor girls, but I never did anything to them. They were projecting on me

---

a peace bond. They need to adhere to certain conditions laid out by the court or face being sent back to prison. The recognizance can be up to 2 years long. The following link provides further information: https://prisonjusticedotorg. files.wordpress.com/2012/11/section-810.pdf

what other people did to them. I really do feel sorry for them. I never touched them."

How do you respond to that level of denial? What can you say that will break through such an utter distortion of the truth?

I turned around and left the room. There was nothing more to say.

Peter was released a few weeks later. A public notification was posted and his section 810 contained over twenty conditions.

Scenario 2

It would be easy to leave the above story just as it is, standing alone. After all, it is a story that fits the public's perception of sex offenders. It is not accurate, however, to paint all sex offenders with the same brush. Over the years, I have dealt with men who were sincerely committed to dealing with their sexual offending and who have been far more honest than Peter. To ensure the above story does not imply this kind of deception is unique to any one demographic of offender, I will share another experience.

It was my last year at Atlantic Institution. I received an email from Neil, a federal chaplain working in a prison in the next province. He was travelling through northern New Brunswick. He wondered if he could drop in to see an inmate who had been transferred to Atlantic a few months earlier. Neil indicated the inmate was someone he had worked closely with prior to his transfer to Atlantic. He knew the family and was connected with them in the community through his parish work.

This was not an unusual request among chaplains. Even so, it did require some verification. I checked with the inmate to see if he knew the chaplain and if he was interested in seeing him. Quickly, he agreed. I then verified where Neil worked and submitted a request for institutional approval to have him come and visit.

The following month, he arrived. I provided office space for them to meet and coordinated movement of the inmate to and from the Chapel. Everything appeared to go well.

A few months later, Neil was travelling through the area to visit family and made the same request. Again, I made arrangements for him to come in.

Four months later, Neil emailed again, wondering if I could again provide a space for him to meet with the inmate. This time he was bringing the inmate's family down to visit the inmate at a Private Family Visit (PFV). The family had little money and no way of travelling to the institution. Neil was providing transportation.

This situation was a bit more unusual. I began to have a few concerns. I could not, however, pinpoint anything, so I put in the requests for clearance and set up a schedule for him to visit in the Chapel.

Neil arrived at the institution and spent the first day visiting with the inmate in the Chapel. The next day, the family had an opportunity to visit him in the PFV. After three days, Neil left with the family and headed back home.

I thought it would be the last time I ever heard anything about Neil. I was mistaken.

Three months after my arrival at Stony Mountain, I received a call from the Security Intelligence Officer at Atlantic Institution.

"Hank, how are things going?"

"Good. Nice to be in a medium. Now, Carl, I know you're not calling to see how I'm doing. Something is up."

"Well, yeah, there is. Do you know the exact dates Neil was in the Chapel?"

"Sure, I'll check my calendar and send the dates off to you shortly. Are you able to let me know what's going on?"

"Sorry. There is an investigation underway. Can't say much."

Alarm bells went off in my mind.

It was another couple of months before I learned what the investigation was about. When I did, the word betrayal seemed inadequate to capture what had unfolded.

Neil was in a relationship with the inmate and had been smuggling drugs into the institution for him. I was the unwitting pawn in a game of lust, drugs, manipulation, and deception.

Dealing with Deception

There is something powerfully insidious about deception. It is the height of self-absorption. For the person using deception to hide their actions, the cost to others, pain inflicted, and eventual consequences do not matter. They cunningly craft a delusion of personal well-being, until they are caught. When chaplains are entangled in deception, it can have a dramatic impact on them, especially on their view of the world they are called to minister in.

A difficult tension emerges out of these experiences. Chaplains are called to live out grace and compassion in a prison world. This requires exercising a certain level of trust and respect with those you minister with. The potential for being lied to, used, and manipulated nevertheless rises with every level of trust you extend. I've found the following insights helpful in navigating this reality.

Taking Off the Rose-Coloured Glasses

No chaplain can escape the reality that there are a few wolves who will show up in their orbit. In fact, they should expect this. After all, it is a prison.

Shortly after the incident with Peter, I happened to express some frustration over his deception to a friend of his who had served time with him. The friend smiled and said, "Hank, everyone lies."

While not a very comforting observation, this carries a good measure of truth, especially in a prison context. The gospel stories of Jesus' betrayal should be a firm reminder of this reality, especially his interactions with Judas.

In the gospel of John, there is an interesting comment about Judas. Jesus has just had his feet anointed with a pint of very expensive perfume. Judas declares, "Why wasn't this perfume sold and the money given to the poor? It is worth a year's wages." (John 12:5)

This sounds like a practical response to such an act. The commentary on Judas' words in the following verse quickly dispel Judas's "practical" response: "He did not say this because he cared about the poor but because he was a thief; as keeper of the money bag, he used to help himself to what was put into it." (John 12:6)

This comment about Judas raises an interesting question. If Jesus knew Judas was a thief and that eventually he would betray him, why did he not send Judas away?

The cynical response would be Jesus needed Judas so the crucifixion would take place as it was prophesied. Judas was nothing more than a tool. I would suggest that was not the case. Instead, I view the relationship between Judas and Jesus as one in which Jesus held open the door for Judas to repent, right up to the last minute.

Whichever way you choose to view Judas' portrayal in the

gospels, there is an important lesson to take away from it. God does not send deceptive people away or prevent them from being part of a church community. You will sometimes find them close to you.

The chaplain's role does not insulate them from being around deceptive people or being deceived. Ignoring this reality will only land a chaplain in trouble.

Learning What Deception Looks Like

There are three areas where a chaplain can learn about the markers of deception. The first is found in relevant books. There are two I can recommend. One has already been mentioned, Gavin DeBecker's *The Gift of Fear*. While a bit dated, his basic principles are solid and the book should be standard reading for every prison chaplain. The second book is a recent release by Malcolm Gladwell, *Talking to Strangers: What We Should Know about the People We Don't Know*. His exploration of truth-default theory is helpful for a prison context. [46]

The next place you can learn about these markers is from staff. Chaplains can wrap themselves into nicely sheltered cocoons. They counsel with someone in the Chapel for an hour and have no other contact with the person outside of a Chapel service. They have no idea what the person sitting in their office is like on the range or in the rest of the institution.

Staff do. Frontline staff see far more of a person than a chaplain does. This is one of the reasons some staff are so cynical regarding Chapel attendance. While they see a saint head off to Chapel, they have to manage the wolf when he comes back to the range. Conversations with Correctional Officers, Parole Officers,

---

[46] Though the whole book is worth reading, see pages 72-79 for discussion related to truth-default theory.

and Psychology are invaluable. These conversations are not about probing for information. They are about listening and observing, as the following example illustrates.

I called an individual down to the Chapel. Within a short time, I received a call from one of the units to deal with an important request. I asked another chaplain if he would let the inmate know I had to step out for a minute. On my return from the unit, I passed through Checkpoint 1. As I did, the female Correctional Officer on duty engaged me in a conversation.

"Hank, I let inmate Sullivan down to the Chapel to see you, but I have to tell you I almost sent him back. Some of his comments to me were derogatory. I would appreciate it if you would have a word with him."

I assured her I would.

I arrived at the Chapel to find John (inmate Sullivan) in a good mood, ready to talk. I waited until a few minutes into our conversation, then asked about his exchange at Checkpoint 1.

His face grew cloudy. "Aw, it was nothing."

"Well, no, it wasn't nothing," I responded.

What followed was a half hour conversation about the impact his interaction had on everyone involved. Staff could easily have sent him back or charged him. They chose to let him come to see me. John had arrived at the Chapel with one face. But he had another face when he interacted with other staff, especially women.

The final place you can learn the markers of deception is from those serving time. The vast majority of inmates will not say a word to you about another inmate. Even so, if they see a serious risk shaping up, you might hear a comment like, "Be careful, chaplain," or, "Maybe you shouldn't be so trusting, chaplain." Pay attention to these comments. They come from individuals who care about you.

Finding a Counterbalance

When deception is revealed, it can have a considerable impact on your ministry. The scenario with Peter was difficult to work through. It left lingering questions about how I should have dealt with him. The pain I witnessed in Ken's life over Peter's deception was unsettling. Should I have intervened sooner? Was there a better way to handle what had happened?

As difficult as Peter's deception was, Neil's deceit left me exceptionally angry. A fellow chaplain, knowing the reality of prison, blatantly used me to access his lover and smuggle drugs in. The inmate in this situation was doing what comes naturally to wolves in prison. He saw an opportunity and jumped at it. That side of the deception was not a surprise to me. But a fellow chaplain? That was deception on another level!

I will always be thankful for the privilege of working with Bo Gajda, my fellow chaplain at Stony Mountain. Bo is a man of sincere compassion, integrity, and wisdom. His friendship proved to be a healing balm to an experience that could have impacted my capacity to work closely with other chaplains.

Encounters with deception need a counterbalance. In the situation with Neil, Bo was my counterbalance, living out the very opposite of Neil's values. In wrestling with Peter's deception, it was working with other men who were travelling the hidden journey and were deeply committed to change, especially one former sex offender, whose insights proved invaluable.

In a world where deceit and lies are commonplace, it would be easy to decide not to trust anyone, especially cons. After all, "Once a con, always a con." But if a chaplain embraces such a worldview, they would be better off finding another area of chaplaincy to work in.

The reality is many of the individuals who come to a chaplain's door are not wolves. To treat everyone that way is unfair and will hamper life-giving ministry. There is a need for balance, to "be as shrewd as snakes and as innocent as doves" (Matthew 10:16).

Violence

As I made my way to the main entrance at Stony Mountain Institution, not even a beautiful blue prairie sky could deflect attention from the unease that lurked within me.

I was scheduled to attend a second Independent Assessment Process Hearing (IAP) for Dylan. An IAP hearing allows victims of abuse at former Canadian residential schools to share their experiences with a neutral adjudicator.[47]

The first one had not gone well. Partway through, it was stopped. It had been gut-wrenching, painful, and difficult.

My unease continued to grow as I walked onto the unit where the second hearing would be held. The Correctional Manager called me over. "Just wanted to let you know Dylan met with his lawyer yesterday. He was not in a good space when he came back to the unit. Not sure what happened between the two of them."

"Thanks. I'll talk to him before we go up to the hearing."

It would be a few minutes before the hearing started, so I moved over to the large window in the dome area of the unit. The window stretched from the floor to ceiling, letting light flood across the unit. Both range barriers were open as men shuffled off to work. A few Correctional Officers were behind the kiosk desk,

---

[47] The following website provides information on the Independent Assessment Process regarding The Indian School Residential Schools Settlement Agreement: http://www.iap-pei.ca/former-ancien/iap/about-eng.php

dealing with inmates as they came off the ranges. It was a typical morning on a prison unit. Gazing out the window, I pondered the path here.

Dylan was a regular at Chapel, often getting staff to call us during the week to see if he could come to the Chapel. We never refused. He would spend some time alone in prayer and then be off to work or back to the unit. For both Bo and I, Dylan had a special place in our hearts. He was a residential school survivor, sitting in prison for a very long time, carrying far more pain than any person should have to shoulder in life.

His request for me to be at his first IAP hearing had come as a surprise. I was a white chaplain. Surely, he wanted someone else, maybe an Elder, or an Indigenous Liaison Officer? "No," he told me the first time. "Just you." When I raised the question a second time, it had clearly upset him that I would ask again. He only wanted me there. I never asked again.

The Hearing today was to take place in a meeting room on the second floor of the unit. His lawyer came down the stairs. "Hi. Dylan and I had a conversation yesterday that didn't go to well."

"So I heard. Do you want to call it off?"

"No. We need to move this process forward."

"Okay, let me go down range and talk to him first."

Walking onto the range, I spotted Dylan sitting at a steel table. I sat down across from him. Before I could say a word, he asked, "Are we ready to go?"

"Yep," I said. "All set."

I didn't get a chance to ask how he was doing. He jumped up from the table and speedily walked toward the open barrier gate. In a split second, I was up, trying to catch up to him. Dylan had a two-foot stick in his hand. As soon as he cleared the barrier, which only took another couple of seconds, he began hurling loud obscenities at his lawyer, stick raised.

The first blow hit the lawyer's hand as he raised it to protect his face. By that point I was right behind Dylan. I grabbed his free hand, pulling it into an armlock. Then, I clasped the stick hand to prevent a second blow from landing. He twisted his head around to see who had a hold of him.

The emotional pain that filled his eyes gave way to shock. I pushed Dylan away and stood between him and the lawyer as he continued to hurl a flurry of insults at his lawyer. Staff quickly moved out from behind the kiosk and surrounded Dylan, ordering him to drop the stick. It took a few firm commands before he finally complied. Through it all, the loud angry insults continued. Dylan was cuffed and taken to segregation.

His lawyer had sustained a bruise to his hand. Medical was called. Range barriers were quickly closed as a small group of inmates gathered on the ranges to see what the commotion was all about.

I stood there for a few minutes, taking in what had just happened. There must be a special grace for chaplains to swear at moments like this. Frustration mixed with anger simmered just below the surface.

The anger wasn't directed at Dylan. Actually, I was thankful I was in the right place at the right time. It could have been far worse. I was angry at all the elements that had brought us to this point. The pain, anguish, and confusion in Dylan's eyes are something that will remain with me.

A year after this incident, I attended a third Hearing with Dylan. By then, he had been transferred to a maximum-security institution. The hearing was completed without incident.

Dealing with Violence

I have faced numerous difficult situations as an inmate and a chaplain. There are any number of violent stories I could have shared for a conversation around this subject of dealing with violence. I chose my experience with Dylan because it is haunting in its clarity and illustrates two of the three insights I can offer chaplains dealing with violence.

Understanding the Cycle of Violence

Violence creates its own cycle, a cycle that repeatedly plays out in a prison environment. Dylan's pain and anguish in life were the direct result of another's violent assault on him—the worst kind, one that rips away your dignity and self-worth, leaving a void of desperate loneliness and brokenness. Cut adrift in a world with no caring emotional anchor, Dylan learned quickly, as others have, that violence was a release button for the rage stoked by what another tore away.

Dylan's angry violence landed him in prison for many years. Here, a lawyer pressed into a well of pain Dylan could barely control. It erupted on a prison unit where I was forced to act and physically restrain him to prevent the cycle from inflicting more pain on another. In my act of restraint, I too exercised a small measure of violence which could easily have escalated to a far worse intervention. His shock, that I would grab him, was enough to prevent a struggle. Had a wrestling match erupted, my next move would not have been as gentle an intervention.

There is something the reader should be aware of before moving on. In all the years I served as a chaplain, this was the only time I physically intervened. I know of no other chaplain who has used a physical intervention. This is not part of a chaplain's calling. I would caution any chaplain thinking about jumping into the fray of a physical altercation in the Chapel or anywhere. You will only get hurt. Violence can happen in seconds. Reacting to it requires skill and training.

Violence permeates every corner of a prison's existence, either overtly or covertly. It rears its destructive head in the broken lives of those whom chaplains minister to, the crimes recounted in their offices, and the victims they deal with. It surfaces in the fear of individuals being muscled for possessions or sex. It erupts in the flexing of power by a gang attempting to control the drug trade. It lashes out in the dark recesses of a prison range where a long-simmering, personal feud is settled with fists or a weapon. It becomes a tool of control when an out-of-control inmate requires Correctional Officers to engage in the use of force, trying to prevent someone else from getting hurt. It is fully visible when an Institutional Emergency Response Team (I.E.R.T.) is suited up in full protective gear, batons and shields at the ready, to quell a disturbance.

As one would expect, the level of violence within a given institution varies. It is much higher in a maximum-security environment. Even medium security environments, however, can experience violence. Minimum-security environments, although far less prone to overt displays of violence, also have their share of covert violence. Some examples are: a sex offender whose food is regularly stolen, a drug trade controlled by a few gang-connected individuals, the consistent verbal harassment and threats made to an inmate who is believed to be an informant.

Throughout this book, I have provided examples of the need for this grounding. From the volunteer who thought making prisons tougher would solve the recidivism problem, to the evangelist who spewed out rage, to the chaplain who accused an inmate of theft in front of his peers, to the chaplain who believed I and another inmate should offer protection, no matter the cost—none of these individuals understood violence and its destructive cycle.

Beware of The Power to Distort

Violence impacts everyone who works or lives in a correctional environment. A person may not see it in action or witness its physical consequences firsthand. But, its reality seeps into conversations, perspectives, and judgements which, in turn, can impact an individual's actions, as the following story illustrates.

It was the height of the biker gang wars in Quebec. Stories of clashes were regularly in the news as two groups in the province fought for control of territory. Some of the action spilled over into the northern part of New Brunswick with affiliate gangs[48] being pulled into the fray. Against this backdrop, Atlantic Institution found itself housing nine members of an affiliate gang in the segregation unit. They had been moved from a local provincial jail amid concerns someone might try and break them out.

It was only a couple of weeks before Christmas. On one of my regular Seg walks, I went down to D range, where the affiliates were being housed. There was no one else on the range as I made my way from cell to cell and introduced myself.

As I stopped at the third locked door, the leader of the group asked if it were possible for them to have Holy Communion on Christmas Eve. I told him pulling everyone out of their cells would probably not go over well with security. I would see if the Roman Catholic Priest, Father John, would be willing to come down to Seg.

---

[48] Affiliate gangs in this situation were motorcycle groups that chose to support one side or the other.

The following Sunday, Father John arrived to hold Mass in the Chapel. He was contracted to work a few hours a week and enjoyed the opportunity to serve in the institution. With an easy-going style and a quick wit, he was well-liked by the men.

After Mass, I approached him and asked if he would be willing to go down to Seg on Christmas Eve to serve Holy Communion. We had a Mass scheduled for that evening anyway. As I explained who the men were, and where they were housed, he stared at me. With a shocked look forming on his face, he asked, "Well, I don't know. Will I be okay there?"

I assured him arrangements would be made with staff, who would also be there, and that everything would be fine. He still didn't seem convinced, but agreed anyway.

The following week, Christmas Eve arrived. After the Mass was over, the men were sent back to their units. I stood at the office door, waiting for Father John to retrieve the Eucharist for the walk down to Seg. Just before we left the Chapel, he asked again, "Are you sure this will be safe?" I quieted his fears with the assurance that everything would be fine.

Our journey was a quiet one, until, halfway down the corridor leading to the Seg unit, Father John asked a third time, "Are you sure we will be okay?" Again, I assured him all would be well.

The barrier gate slowly moved open, then shut behind us as we stepped onto the unit. One of the officers greeted us as we walked down the steps to the barrier gate on D Range. By this time, Father John was visibly uncomfortable as the gate whined open and slammed behind us.

The officer looked at me. "Hank, I'm going to pop the food slots open. As you give out communion, close the slots."

"No problem. I can do that."

The officer moved down the range, opening the food slots. Much to the dismay of Father John, the officer left the range.

What Father John didn't understand or appreciate was that the officers were giving us the space to hold a service. They could easily observe us from the control post.

That is not what Father John saw. He looked abandoned. His apprehension was evident as he shot a worried look my way. I approached the first cell, bent down at the food slot, shook the individual's hand, and introduced Father John. Hesitating at first, Father John offered communion to the man and then a quick prayer. As he finished, I came up behind him and closed the food slot.

By the time Father John reached the third cell, a strange thing began to happen. Bending over to peer through the food slot, he started to talk more. As we moved down the range, the time he spent at each cell continued to increase. Here we were on Christmas Eve, in a maximum-security unit, offering Holy Communion to a bunch of outlaw bikers. It is one of those scenes you don't forget.

Forty minutes later, we left the range. I stopped in at the unit office to thank staff for giving us some space. We exited the unit. On our walk back to the Chapel, clearly relieved everything had gone well, Father John made a comment that left me silent. "Hank, they were just ordinary normal men who sincerely appreciated us coming to see them."

Rudyard Kipling once remarked, "Of all the liars in the world, sometimes the worst are our own fears." In a prison world, it is easy to allow fear to craft everything else except ordinary normal human beings. Fear, encouraged by the violence spoken about or witnessed, can easily distort our view of people by shaping them into monsters.

If the man standing in front of you is framed as a monster, then he automatically becomes less than human. As a result, almost by reflex, he gets treated with less dignity and respect than another.

Inmates can smell fear in staff. A few will take full advantage of it when the opportunity presents itself.

Fear is a well-used tactic in prison. In the wrong hands, it can be masterfully employed to bend and twist someone to do another's beckoning.

From one who has served time, I would offer the following warning. Inmates can also smell a chaplain's judgements. No number of nice smiles, kind words, or gentle manner will cover over the contempt a chaplain may hold toward an inmate. Sooner or later, those judgements will surface in a comment, mannerism, or lack of response to a request, alerting an inmate to a chaplain who believes they are superior to their fellow human being who is serving time.

Finding Sanctuary

After the altercation with Dylan, I travelled back through the institution, stopping in at the medium-security chaplains' offices to ask if I could use a computer. I had to write an Observation Report detailing the incident. Within a few minutes, I was finished.

I went up to the main Correctional Manager's office to drop off the report. While there, I spent a few minutes talking with staff about the incident, then moved through the hallway and gates that led to the Main Entrance. I had to see to a few matters in the minimum unit, which was adjacent to the medium.

Just before I exited the building, one of the Correctional Managers caught up with me and asked, "Hank, are you okay?"

I wasn't quite sure how to answer that question. There were too many confusing thoughts running through my head to offer a coherent response. I simply said, "Yeah, I'm okay," not meaning a word of it.

She was unconvinced. Years of being a Correctional Officer had trained her to pay attention to everything that went along with the words.

As I walked over to the minimum, the blue prairie sky received none of my attention. Instead, I was gazing within, trying to sort through my rambling thoughts. Approaching the minimum administrative building I looked up and was startled to see one of the Correctional Officers standing on the top steps just outside the door. Someone had called ahead.

As I approached, he looked at me with concern. "Hank, are you okay?"

This time there was no pat answer. "No. I'm not. I need to get out of here and take some time for myself." We spent a few minutes talking, all of which I deeply appreciated.

I headed back to my office, then called my former chaplaincy counterpart at Stony Mountain, Bo Gajda, asking if he had some time to spare that afternoon. Bo had retired from chaplaincy a year earlier.

I grabbed my backpack, headed over to the main building to sign out, and handed in the Chapel keys. Again, a couple of staff checked in with me.

Forty minutes later, I found myself in Bo's backyard, sitting on a garden swing, this time taking in the beautiful clear blue prairie sky.

For the next couple of hours, Bo graciously sat and listened as I unloaded my fatigue, frustrations, and concerns—all intermingled with a healing conversation around faith and the future.

I share this to highlight two things. First, in a correctional environment, with many things going on, including other situations to manage, frontline correctional staff took the time to check in and see how I was doing.

Why would they express that level of concern? The answer is as simple as it is profound.

Of all the staff who work in a prison, frontline staff are acutely aware of the impact incidents can have on a person's life, no matter how small the event may appear. Mine was a very minor incident if measured on a scale of violence—I have faced far worse. But its impact was considerable.

It is important to pay close attention to your personal experiences with violence. They can affect your life in unforeseen ways. The staff you work with in a prison setting are aware of this fact.

The second item to highlight flows from the first. There are many good resources available for dealing with stress and trauma.[49] Over my years of serving as a chaplain, these resources were helpful in working through difficult incidents. Overarching all these resources, however, is a concept and practice I have found invaluable for managing encounters with violence: crafting sanctuary.

Sanctuary is a place where you are safe. When I use the word safe, it not only incorporates the experience of physical safety but also the need to "feel safe".

It is an important nuance to understand. Father John's short trip to segregation provides insight in highlighting the difference. As we left the Chapel and walked down toward the Seg unit, he was very concerned about his safety. Yet, there was never a serious risk of harm. I was with him, staff were on hand, cell doors were locked, and the bikers had no intention of hurting him. The environment was safe. The people he was with were safe. Despite all this, he did not "feel safe". It took twenty minutes of

---

[49] The following is a link to an organization that has proven helpful in the past. There are numerous others to choose from: https://headington-institute.org/overview

interaction with men behind steel doors and no adverse actions before he began to feel safe. You can be in a very safe place, but not feel safe at all.

These sanctuaries can be crafted in different places. For myself, family and certain friends are at the top of the list.

I also find sanctuary in a place where others would expect exactly the opposite: on a motorcycle. When I am out on the open road, with a small tent and sleeping bag strapped to the back of a bike, there is no safer place for me to be. I have had some of my deepest conversations with God on these road trips. I return home refreshed and ready to take on whatever new work lays before me.

Sanctuaries not only provide a safe place to be, they enable a person to reflect, integrate difficult experiences, seek direction, and be refreshed.

As Bo and I sat together talking about the event that had unfolded with Dylan, it wasn't the physical altercation that was under discussion. It was the implications of the event. I am a lifer on parole for the rest of my life. I have conditions on parole I am required to abide by, and a parole officer I meet with regularly. The altercation that day raised a highly sensitive issue for any lifer on parole: a physical altercation. I found myself wrestling with an inmate in a federal prison, a situation that could have escalated quickly. There could have been a real risk to my personal freedom if I would have used more force.

Our conversation did not revolve around whether I would be physically safe working in a prison. It weaved through the risks I was taking with my personal freedom working in a prison environment.

As a chaplain who has talked with lifers sent back to prison for various reasons, I was well aware of the thin line someone walks serving a life sentence on parole. I could not have had such a personal conversation with someone else. I needed an individual

I could trust, someone I felt safe expressing very personal reflections with. These were deep waters, requiring a friendship that understood the issues of the Corrections and chaplaincy world.

11. Seasons

There is a time for everything,
and a season for every activity under heaven.
(Ecclesiastes 3:1)

My first introduction to what some would term "burnout"[50] came while I was still an inmate working at the Chapel in Springhill Institution. Father Bob, the Catholic Chaplain, had left the institution to be replaced by another priest, Father Jim. From the first day Father Jim arrived, it was evident he was the direct opposite of our former chaplain. He was abrupt, demeaning to inmates, and spent little time at the institution. When Father Jim was challenged on specific issues, he instantly reverted to a superior attitude. Inmates were expected to take direction, not ask questions. His Masses were particularly memorable. He would race into the institution, sometimes late,

---

[50] The World Health Organization defines burnout as, "resulting from chronic workplace stress that has not been successfully managed. It is characterized by three dimensions:
- feelings of energy depletion or exhaustion
- increased mental distance from one's job, or feelings of negativism or cynicism related to one's job
- reduced professional efficacy
  Burn-out refers specifically to phenomena in the occupational context and should not be applied to describe experiences in other areas of life."

quickly run through the Mass, and a few minutes later hurriedly exit the Chapel, offering some excuse or other as he left.

This is another memory that would have slipped into oblivion had it not been for two experiences connected to it. The first was the way he treated a Sister at the institution, who was also a chaplain. His abruptness and superior attitude took on a whole new dimension when he dealt with her. It was very difficult to watch, especially considering this particular Sister had earned a great deal of respect with the men.

The second was just as disturbing. Father Jim, who claimed to be a Charismatic Catholic, had connections with a Christian television program of the day. One Sunday afternoon he appeared on the program. While being interviewed, he expounded on all the wonderful things he was doing at Springhill Institution. This was in stark contrast to the reality unfolding within the confines of the prison. He was never around, so nobody could see him, except for a couple of favourite inmates. When he was there, his uncaring attitude soon earned him a negative reputation.

He didn't last long. There was a huge sigh of relief the day he resigned and left for other parish work.

After he left, I was deeply perplexed about his actions. When he arrived, we were told he had been a chaplain in another prison out west and knew his way around a jail. Yet, he hated being in a prison, and had little regard for the struggles and difficulties inmates faced serving time. It was not until years later, after witnessing others taking the same general course, or hearing about similar experiences, that I began to appreciate the reality of burnout in prison chaplaincy.

For a few there can be dramatic consequences for not dealing with burnout. They end up losing a grip on their moral compass, like one chaplain I recall who was walked off the prison property by security, accused of smuggling drugs in for one of the biker gangs. Chaplains can start out their ministry with the best of intentions, only to have the negative experiences of prison, especially deception and violence, hammer away at their hold on that compass.

Sometimes, the decision to exit chaplaincy can be difficult, especially for those of us who have invested a great deal of energy and time in the ministry. In this closing chapter I would like to share my personal exit from chaplaincy, a few helpful insights I have gained in the process, and closing thoughts for those who might wish to follow.

Knowing When to Leave

From the beginning of my work training chaplains, I have provided this simple yet difficult piece of advice—know when it is time to leave. There are some chaplains who can survive in prison chaplaincy for many years, while others do not. I would suggest there are two reasons for this.

First, depending on the type of institutions a chaplain serves in, they may experience a significant number of traumatic events during their tenure. These can limit the lifespan of one's chaplaincy. We can only take so much before the capacity to integrate experiences begins to overwhelm us. There is a finite threshold we need to be aware of, a threshold that is different for everyone. On the rare occasion, a chaplain may start work in an institution and resign shortly thereafter. I have heard of a couple of situations where a new chaplain resigned the same day they started. There is absolutely no shame in that call. They, fortunately, realized the danger of staying before something bad happened.

The second reason is, we all bring our past to work with us. No one escapes the experiences that have formed them. For instance, if you have been the victim of violence and abuse, it can cast a long shadow in your life, even if you have spent time working through the damage. There is a powerful, visceral experience that can occur when your past meets a perpetrator in the present, something that can happen regularly in prison. An example may help.

At the age of sixteen, I quit school and began work on a CN rail gang in Northern Ontario. I was a skinny kid, immersed in drugs, who didn't know much about life. Rail gang teams usually spent the week working on a section of track. We were housed in bunk rail cars coupled to a kitchen car and a few supply cars. Occasionally, we would be shunted onto a siding near a town.

One evening, one of the men on our crew returned to the bunk car very drunk. He burst into the room I was sharing with a new crew member, grabbed me, fired a fist into my face and threw me into the corner. The moment I tried to move out of the corner he would hammer me with another solid hit. I weighed a paltry 160 pounds compared to his 220 pounds of hardened muscle. For hours, I sat in the corner. If I spoke, I was hit. If I moved, I was hit. Finally, in the early hours of the morning, he stumbled off to his bunk in another car.

I never reported the event. I was too embarrassed. Instead, I let it build a rage within me. I made a vow: *No one will ever do that to me again.* That experience, along with a few others, no doubt contributed to the foundation on which my rebellious path was built.

When I began work in chaplaincy, this experience reared its head on more than one occasion. After all, prison has lots of bullies and violent men in it. You cannot sit with a young man who is being muscled on his range and not feel your emotions yanked up from the distant past. It takes hard work to keep your emotions in check, especially if you have served time and witnessed numerous men hammered into submission.

In sharing this experience, it is important to recognize such events, when worked through, can also prove helpful inside the walls.

Jake was serving time for murder, and, as part of his case management plan, he was required to attend what was then termed a High Intensity Violence Prevention Program. It was being taught by two female staff.

After a Chapel service, which Jake rarely attended, I asked him how the program was going. A scowl spread across his scarred face. He was a big man, quite capable of extreme violence.

He responded, "Not that well."

I decided to prod a bit. "Is it tougher than you thought it would be?"

The scowl was quickly overshadowed by a twist of anger. "They shouldn't let people like that teach the program."

He had my full attention. "What kind of people?"

Leaning a bit closer, intent on catching my eye, he said, "You know what I mean. She is a victim."

The conversation ended as an officer opened the Chapel door for inmates to go back to the unit.

Jake thought he was going to enjoy a cake walk through the program. After all, most of his life had been built on intimidating people. Surely, a couple of women could easily be intimidated.

Instead, what he encountered was a lead instructor who wasn't fazed by his intimidation tactics. He ran up against someone who was more than willing to push him on issues he needed to face. Jake had not bargained for a 110-pound dynamo, whose experiences in life had long ago knocked off any pretence of providing feel-good therapy sessions for someone of his character. She didn't tell him she was a victim. She didn't have to. He knew it because of the way she handled him.

My own past struggles were churning in the background as I conversed with Bo after the incident with Dylan. I wondered,

Have I reached the threshold? I began to face a reality, which my wife Linda had expressed on more than one occasion. Perhaps it was time to take my advice and "know when it is time to leave".

Over the next few months, I mulled over my exit from chaplaincy. The opportunity came via an unexpected path.

Friendship

It was the Spring of 2014. The year prior had been busy as I submitted a thesis for my Doctor of Ministry, continued to teach a course at Booth University College, and worked as a full-time Chaplain at the Stony Mountain Institution Minimum Unit. I was looking forward to graduation. The Doctor of Ministry had turned into a six-year adventure. I was glad it would all come to a close soon.

At the same time, Kairos Pneuma Chaplaincy Inc. was ramping up their organization. After winning a small contract for federal prison chaplaincy services in British Columbia in October 2013, they had gone on to bid on the national contract in early 2014 and won. They were now busy looking for staff throughout the country.

Although I had been involved in the initial discussions about forming KPCI, I chose not to continue my involvement, simply because of the workload I was carrying. I had nourished a dream to do research on grief and loss in prison populations and earn a Doctor of Ministry. I did not want to lose that opportunity.

I remember when the call came in. I was driving down Main Street in Winnipeg, just going past the Salvation Army Booth Centre. I was thinking over the conversation I had with Bo after the incident with Dylan the summer prior. I was now graduating with a Doctor of Ministry. Perhaps it was time to seriously look at other opportunities, such as a return to pastoral ministry, maybe teaching, or something completely different.

The Bluetooth in the car signalled a call. I looked at the number and knew who it was. This was a call I needed to take.

"Hi, John, how are you doing?"

"Good, Hank. Really busy of course with all the work ahead of us." John Tonks was the President of KPCI, but more than that, a close friend.

We first met in Springhill Institution while I was serving time. He was a volunteer attending the Marathon Groups in the Chapel. Over the years John had gone on to be a Chaplain at Springhill Institution, then Regional Chaplain for the Atlantic Region, and finally, the Associate Director of Chaplaincy at National Headquarters in Ottawa before retiring. Intermittently, we would cross each other's path, until I became the Chaplain at Atlantic Institution. Then, John became my boss, so to speak. One particular incident sealed our friendship.

It was about a year and a half after the riots at Atlantic Institution. The decision was made by the federal chaplaincy department in Ottawa to drop the chaplaincy complement at the institution down from two to one. After two years at the prison, I found myself working alone in an environment still wrestling through disturbances and difficult staff management relations. I was stressed to the limit when John came to see how I was doing. I was thinking of leaving chaplaincy.

At this time, John was the Regional Chaplain. He sat with me in the Chaplain's office as I let loose months of suppressed emotions, anger and resentment pouring out over the loss of a good partner in ministry and the chaos in the institution.

I finished my rant, exhausted. I looked at John, not knowing what to expect.

His face was filled with pain. His eyes grew moist. And then, he said something I have never forgotten. "Hank, we never intended for this to happen to you."

John could have said a number of things to me that day, from, "Suck it up, buttercup," to, "It's probably time to leave." Instead, his words conveyed a deep care and understanding of the struggle I was facing as an ex-con trying to manage ministry in a Max alone. That encounter would seal a friendship that has lasted for over twenty-five years.

It felt a bit like being back in that office, as I took John's call on my Bluetooth, still driving through the streets of Winnipeg.

"So, what's up John?" I asked.

"Well, we were wondering if you might be willing to take care of the Prairie Region for us. We need a Regional Manager. I know we are asking a lot here. There are no guarantees on what the future holds. I know you will want to talk with Linda first before you respond."

The term no-brainer came to mind. "John, I am in. Linda and I have already been talking about my leaving chaplaincy."

In April, 2014, I left prison chaplaincy and began work with KPCI. The remainder of the year saw a flurry of changes in my work life as I shifted gears to supervising chaplains. Along the way, John taught me the finer points and pitfalls of contracting services, and Lloyd Bruce, who was Secretary at KPCI, taught me valuable lessons in organization. Lloyd is an organizational genius. His capacity to run the administrative side of KPCI was amazing to watch.

I suspect my early experiences of wrestling through my conversion experience alone, along with being a youth devoid of any solid connections, laid the groundwork for the value I place on friendships. I have come to discover that along with my faith, there is no greater gift God has provided in my life than the close friendships that have helped define my journey. These have proven crucial in any decisions I have made, for one simple reason. Close friends usually see things in our lives we can't see.

Before my release from prison, I was determined to go into ministry, but I believed counselling was the path God had laid out for me. One particular conversation with Dennis Veinotte, who was the Protestant Chaplain at Springhill Institution and another of my significant mentors, still brings a smile to my face.

I was out on an eight-hour escorted pass in the community to speak at a church and share my story. After the service, we were sitting together on the steps of the entrance to the church, soaking in the afternoon sun.

"So, Hank, have you thought about perhaps looking at pastoral ministry?" Dennis asked.

I looked at him like he had two heads. "Are you nuts? Do you know how long that will take? Seven years of school! I will be an old man by that time!" My youthful 27-year-old brain had done a quick calculation. By the time I would be released from prison, complete an undergraduate degree and Master of Divinity degree, along with at least one year of internship, I would enter pastoral ministry an old, greying 38-year-old! I was not having any of that.

Dennis smiled, knowingly. "Well, maybe just think about it."

After my release from prison, I eventually relented to his advice. However, it was not until I completed my first year of Seminary (four years into my educational journey) that I began to realize the wisdom of Dennis's words. He had observed gifts in me I did not see within myself at the time.

Close personal friendships hold up a reflection for us. Our close friends are often free to speak to us about things others would not. They are prepared to walk with us as we wrestle with trying to understand the path God is directing us on. Often, I have found friendships working in tandem with my prayer life as

I attempted to discern where I should go and what I should do. This has been especially true in conversations with my best friend of all, Linda.

Friendships have proven to be lifegiving for me. They have challenged me when I wasn't seeing straight, offered gentle reminders about what is important in life, provided a space to explore what the future may hold, and helped me to discern when it might be time to leave.

"Prepared in Advance"

It was a cool spring afternoon in March, 2016, as I gazed out through the windows of the Johnston Terminal at The Forks in Winnipeg, Manitoba. There weren't many people around as I sat nursing a hot Americano. I watched the clouds float through a bright blue sky and thought, *What a perfect picture of my life right now. Clouds, drifting on currents of wind, uncertain about where they are going, unsure of the path their future holds.*

My professional working life had come to a screeching halt in a fashion I never expected. For two years, 2014–2016, I had poured mountains of time, energy, and experience into helping KPCI run well. We had broken new ground with innovative, professional services, doing something no one believed we could pull off. Then, we lost the chaplaincy contract. It was difficult to accept, but even more difficult letting go of the dream we had nourished.

Again, I gazed at the clouds drifting by, thinking to myself, *Where am I going? What will I do? Who wants a 59-year-old ex-con pastor?*

Sitting there, lost in thought, I wondered what God was planning to do with his tired, worn-out servant. The future looked uncomfortably blank for a man who enjoyed hitting the ground running, and always had goals to strive for.

As I sat there, my cell phone buzzed with a call.

"Hank, it's Glenn."

"Hi, Glenn. What's up?" Glenn was the Program Director at Open Circle, a prison visitation program here in Winnipeg.

"Well," he said, "I heard you might be available. Would you be willing to head up Open Circle for a few months? I need to take some time off."

We talked about his situation and what was needed for the job. It was a perfect fit. I laid the phone down and shook my head. A smile began to emerge as I thought about what had just happened. A passage of Scripture began rolling through my mind:

"For we are God's handiwork, created in Christ Jesus to do good works, which God prepared in advance for us to do." (Ephesians 2:10)

A few months later, I received a phone call from John Tonks. He confessed that when the contract ended, his greatest concern was for those of us who made up the KPCI management team. He worried about where we would land. Would we be okay? This not only spoke about John's heart and care for us, but for me, it also brought Ephesians 2:10 into sharper focus. I was worried about what the future held, and John was even more concerned, yet there, in the wonder of Scripture, was a promise God has repeatedly fulfilled.

I suspect one of the reasons a few chaplains continue to labour in prison ministry long past the day they should have left is because of a fear over what lays beyond the walls regarding future work and ministry. This is understandable. If you have invested so much in a ministry, it can be difficult to look beyond it and see yourself in a very different role. This difficulty can be compounded if your position is one in civil service, with pension, benefits, and a good salary, a situation that exists in a few provinces in Canada. However, even in these situations I would offer a word of caution.

A couple of years after I left chaplaincy, my son Isaac remarked, "You know, Dad, you are a lot more relaxed since you left chaplaincy."

That was convicting. I thought, *Man, what was I like before?*

I mentioned Isaac's comment to Linda. She smiled.

In ministry, it is easy to wrap ourselves up so tightly in the work that we lose sight of the bigger picture, how it may be impacting both ourselves and others.

Those who have served as prison chaplains and transitioned into other forms of ministry often bring with them a deep compassion for the most despised in our society. For many of them, the work of chaplaincy has pulled back the curtain on human suffering, struggle, and God's grace. It changes you. That capacity to see the world differently is one of the greatest gifts former chaplains bring back into the ministries they engage in on the street. I know it has a profound impact on both my work as Program Director of Open Circle and now as an Executive Director.

There will always be work in the kingdom of God for those who are open to it. As I reflect on my journey, each phrase in Ephesians speaks to God's incredible grace at work.

Who would have thought that a nineteen-year-old drug addict facing life for murder was "God's workmanship"? Who could have imagined I would be "created in Christ Jesus to do good works"? And, I could never have dreamed of the works which "God prepared in advance" for me to do.

Full Circle

Gordon Green and I have known each other since my time as a chaplain at Atlantic Institution. He was a volunteer coming into the institution and started a Community Chaplaincy in Miramichi, New Brunswick. A few years later, Gordon would become a chaplain at Atlantic and then move on to do chaplaincy at Springhill Institution in Nova Scotia. We share a deep faith in Jesus Christ, a care for those we minister with, and a passion for motorcycling.

I eventually moved to Winnipeg to work at Stony Mountain Institution, and even though we were separated by a few thousand kilometres, we stayed in touch. In 2009, federal chaplaincy decided to hold their quadrennial conference in Vancouver, Canada. Gordon and I made plans to go. He would ride out from the east, cutting across the northern US to Winnipeg where he would meet me. We would then continue on to the conference. It was a journey which only a couple of passionate motorcyclists could have enjoyed.

Before he arrived, Gordon hit a snag south of the border in North Dakota. His bike quit running. The suspected problem was bad gas, but there wasn't much he could do about it where he was. Fortunately for us, and especially Gordon, there was an active chapter of the Christian Motorcycle Association here in Winnipeg at the time. After a few phone calls, one of the members agreed to go down to North Dakota and trailer him across the Canada/US Border up to Winnipeg.

You would think such an experience would have slowed us down. Not a chance. After a trip to the Harley dealer, another small miracle later, we were set for a trip to British Columbia.

We left Winnipeg the last week of May in single digit temperatures. By the time we hit Brandon, two hours down the road, light puffy snowflakes were descending from above. We pulled in to fuel up and grab a bite to eat.

As we sat down warming our hands with a cup of hot coffee, I looked at Gordon. "It's snowing! Are we a bit nuts?"

A huge grin spread across his face, and then we both broke out in laughter.

"Of course we are," he said, "but I would not want to be anywhere else."

Soon we were on the road again. Within a few hours the weather had warmed considerably and by 11:00 p.m. that night we had reached Crowsnest Pass, exactly 1,534 kilometres from my home in Winnipeg. We had run all day, sixteen and a half hours, with only a few stops, enjoying the open road.

Gordon had family in Crowsnest Pass and we were very thankful they had arranged for us to stay at a cabin belonging to a friend. We parked the bikes, unpacked, and were soon sound asleep.

The next morning provided one of the most memorable moments in all my years of riding. It was 5:00 a.m. I was slowly waking up. The excitement of taking my first ride through the mountains had pulled me from my sleep. I could hear Gordon stirring.

"Hank! Are you awake?"

"Yep, sure am."

Then he spoke a line I will always remember. Not because it was profound, but because it simply underlined the joy we both experienced on such a journey.

"You want to go riding?"

"You bet. Let's roll!"

Within a few minutes we were dressed, guiding our bikes away from the house. It was now 5:30 in the morning. Once we were well away from the neighbourhood and on the open road, we cranked our bikes over. Gordon's Harley thundered to life.

We hopped on and travelled down to a local restaurant we knew was open early.

After a good breakfast and a quick visit with family, we were on the road. We didn't stop. It was too beautiful to get off the bikes.

It was a perfect day for riding, the right temperature and a deep blue sky above. As we crossed over mountains, dipping into valleys and swerving through the many beautiful curves of Highway 3, we enjoyed a little taste of heaven. It is hard to convey what it is like, riding through the midst of God's incredible creation with a fellow brother in Christ, soaking up the freedom that comes from having two wheels anchored on a steel frame and a hundred horsepower under you.

We arrived in Vancouver that same day. What a trip it was. After the conference, we travelled throughout BC. We visited numerous places, met many people, and enjoyed the sheer joy of being alive in Jesus Christ.

One of these stops was where I had my first face-to-face meeting with Brian and Marilyn Scott. Just like my life, Gordon's hadn't been a pretty picture until he came to faith. Riding in such freedom was a celebration for both of us, a reminder we had been blessed with a new life.

This past year, as Gordon and I spent some time talking about life, bikes, ministry, and aging, our conversation flowed toward the changes in prison chaplaincy and his work in chaplaincy. He too had left when the new contractor took over chaplaincy.

"You know," he said, "that was for a season in my life."

Gordon's observation that prison chaplaincy was for a season in his life brought me full circle, back to a struggle I began this book with, as I faced the wall of resistance each time I tried to write it:

"Who is pushing me to pierce the wall, God or man?"

It was never just one or the other. It was both. In his letter to the Philippian Church, Paul writes, "for it is God who works in you to will and to act according to his good purpose." (Philippians 2:13)

As this truth began to sink in, I realized my personal journey of faith and wrestling it on to paper was not just meant to provide helpful guidance to chaplains. It had a calling far beyond that.

It is my hope that the stories, experiences, and reflections on God's incredible ways may not only encourage those presently in chaplaincy, but also speak to those who may be considering, for a season of their life, ministering in prison, whether as a chaplain or a volunteer.

I also pray all that is contained in this book may provide hope to those who long for a new life in Jesus Christ—whether you are in prison or not—and courage to trust and follow our Lord's calling, wherever it will take you.

Epilogue

Ted's Story

Throughout my years of serving as a prison chaplain, I had the privilege of working with many dedicated people. Out of all these experiences, there is one story I would like to conclude with.

Just like many who come to minister in prison, Ted Sawchuk's journey took an interesting route. After thirty years of working for Environment Canada, he retired and started searching for more opportunities to serve God. Ted was already involved with Promise Keepers Canada, a parachurch organization founded to work specifically with men. His deep care for men who were struggling in life was foundational to what he wanted to continue doing with his life. Eventually, he was hired by the Salvation Army's Correctional and Justice Services to provide outreach work in prisons around Winnipeg.

I met Ted while I was a chaplain at Stony Mountain. Every Monday, he would come to the institution to see men and lead the Salvation Army worship service. Quickly, I realized there was something different about him. His deep compassion for those serving time, and an unusual thirst to learn how to effectively work in prison, made him stand out.

We spent many hours talking about ministry, working together to provide care for men in prison and those being released into the community. Ted went on to pursue further education as he continued his work with the Salvation Army. In

2014, as I moved into a new role as Regional Manager for Chaplaincy Services for KPCI, one of my first tasks was to find quality chaplains for prison vacancies. We hired Ted as our chaplain at the minimum unit at Stony Mountain Institution.

During his time there, Ted provided exceptional pastoral services. Thirty years of working in government furnished Ted with a built-in skillset for dealing with the bureaucracy of a prison environment. His gracious care for all those he met, both inmate and staff, won him high praise.

Unfortunately, when the new contractor took over the chaplaincy contract in 2016, they did not hire Ted. For me, it was one of the more perplexing moments in the transition. When men at the prison learned Ted would not be returning as a chaplain, a petition was started, requesting he be hired back. It received over three hundred inmate signatures—quite a testament to the impact he had.

Ted was not sidelined for long. As Program Director of Open Circle, I suggested we hire Ted part time to do work with men who were transitioning into the community. At the same time, Ted went back to work part time for the Salvation Army. It was a perfect fit. Within a short period of time, Ted was back doing what he did best—ministering to men in and out of prison.

Sadly, it would not last. In the fall of 2017, Ted went into hospital for what was supposed to be a routine surgery to repair his knee. A few days later, on October 29, 2017, he passed away.

Ted's loss hit me particularly hard. We shared more than a friendship. We shared a calling, a vision, a longing to make the world a better place by reaching out to those who many did not want anything to do with. We shared conversations filled with laughter, questions, struggles, and above all, hope. We encouraged each other in our walk of faith. He was a brother, a fellow companion on a road few travel.

In wrestling with this deep loss, I penned the following poem.

Ode to a Fellow Companion

You walked through the passage of Stony's steel gates,
with a call on your life, you claimed was from God.
I'd heard it before, those eloquent words,
that in the pit of a prison oft crumbled away.

"What are you made of?" I thought to myself.
"Did you arrive here to care, or to judge and condemn?"
Harsh thoughts you may think,
   from a time-worn chaplain,
who'd seen his fair share of the desperate and broken.

Harsh they may seem, time tested they are.
Not all who arrive with a call from above,
weigh the price they must pay to follow the path.
More often than not they just fall away.

You found this realm behind Stony's steel gates,
challenging your views, your thoughts about God.
I watched as you wrestled, and struggled to find,
your place in this world, so alien to most.

Then you did something so few ever do.
You came and you asked,
"What should I do, to live out this call?
What must I do, to honour the One whose voice I hear?"

Long hours were spent exploring the call.
I showed you three things that this path would require.
Each with its challenges, each with its toll,
with the third by far, the place where most fall.

The first was to learn from the travelled and worn,
whose lives spoke of seeking a way through the dark.
Deny their wisdom and you bring no light,
you simply become, a loud sounding gong.

Next is to remember and never forget,
no matter the place one crafted in life,
all carry the likeness of the One who gave life.
In the calling you live, *us vs them* lay no claim.

The third, by far, takes the greatest of tolls,
caring for those who, many would call, lower than low.
To do this your heart must be stretched and grow,
shaped and formed by the Master's hand.

When this you can do, and turn no one away,
you will walk in the calling, you claimed from above.
A path well-travelled by others before,
a calling that changes a man to a saint.

You listened intently to the challenge laid out.
With no sounds of objection, no excuses to offer,
you pulled on this mantel of God's holy call,
and walked through the passage of Stony's steel gates.

No matter how hopeless and desperate life seemed,
you opened your heart to any who came.
When challenged and mocked you quietly said,
"We are all crafted in the image of the Maker of life."

The lowest of the low found compassion and care.
Many came with their burdens and pain.
It was not long before others would learn,
of a man who could turn no one away.

Moments of doubt would spring from within,
"Do I honour my Lord, or do I fall short?
Surely there are others, with great knowledge and skill,
whose service would be far better than mine."

I think it is the nature of truly great men,
to be blind to the light they shine through their life.
They question and wonder, unsure of the gift,
so evident to see, behind Stony's steel gates.

My brother in faith, if only you knew,
how great was your gift, to the many you touched.
Surely, our Lord is now honouring your call,
when you walked through the passage of
   Stony's steel gates.
     (November 25, 2017)

On November 5th, Ted's funeral took place at The Salvation Army Heritage Park Temple. The church could barely contain all the people who showed up to pay their respects. There was standing room only in the sanctuary, and back through to the entrance of the building. Ted's legacy filled a house of worship to overflowing.

There were people from all walks of life, including a small group of men who had served time. We stood together at the back of the church, quietly reflecting, immensely thankful, that for a season, God had allowed Ted to grace our lives.

> The Spirit of the Lord is on me,
>> because he has anointed me
>> to preach good news to the poor.
> He has sent me to proclaim freedom for the prisoners
>> and recovery of sight for the blind,
> to release the oppressed,
>> to proclaim the year of the Lord's favor.
>>> (Luke 4:18-19)

Acknowledgements

In writing a story that spans over forty-five years of prison, Corrections, and ministry experience, it is impossible to include everyone who has been part of my journey of faith. Of those who are not mentioned within the stories in this book, there are a few to whom I would like to express my gratitude.

When I arrived at Springhill Institution as an inmate, Dennis Veinotte was the Protestant chaplain. In the latter years of my sentence and after my release, Dennis's friendship became a significant part of my life. After leaving chaplaincy, he went on to become Professor of Clinical Pastoral Education at Acadia Divinity College. His mentorship through school, the ordination process, and pastoral ministry were vital to my growth. I spent many hours visiting with Dennis and Connie at their home in Wolfville, Nova Scotia. Dennis passed away in 2012. Thank you, Connie, for the warm hospitality that has always been there when I arrived. It was so very welcome.

As this book reveals, it has been the nature of my walk with the Lord that the mentors and friends God has brought into my life have sometimes come from unexpected places. Glen Manthorne was one of them. Glen was my Case Management Officer in Springhill Institution. After my release, we continued to stay in touch. Glen's wife, Ann, and I had also formed a very special friendship. She could speak truth to me like no one else. I, in turn, could talk with her about things I could not speak to others about. One of the most humbling moments in my life was when Ann passed away. I attended the funeral and the family insisted I sit with them as a family member. Thank you, Glen, Christiann, George, and Glen junior. I still miss her.

Added to those mentioned above, I believe it is also important to acknowledge the denomination that provided the opportunity for me to minister, the Canadian Baptists of Atlantic

Canada. Ordination, the act of being set apart for ministry, is not only a personal call. It is the Body of Jesus Christ, the church, acknowledging, agreeing with, and affirming God's call on your life.

It is a profoundly healing experience when a community reaches out to an individual, dresses their wounds, helps them stand, and restores that which was lost. I had no community, until one gathered around me. For a man who was an outcast, a former criminal, it is still deeply humbling to be given a place to belong and minister. I want to especially acknowledge Rev. John Beers, who was the Area Minister and supervised my first pastoral charge. Thank you, John, for the trust you placed in me.

When chaplaincy work eventually took me to Winnipeg, Manitoba, the Canadian Baptists of Western Canada willingly accepted my credentials to minister, offering the same community and support I experienced in Eastern Canada. I want to especially thank Bob Krahn, Clarke Gietz, Ken Thiessen, the late David Holten, and Mark Doerksen for the many conversations, wisdom, and friendship that helped me feel at home in the denomination.

As my life has not been shaped in isolation, neither has this book. I would like to thank Dr. Dan Schellenberg for his invaluable feedback on the manuscript. Years of being a Parole Officer, and now a psychologist, positioned him well to occasionally challenge my viewpoints and observations.

Along with Dan I would like to thank John Tonks for his help in talking through the initial chapters of the manuscript. Bo Gajda and Don Stoesz also provided many helpful insights out of their years of experience as prison chaplains. Added to this, Sheila MacCrimmon's assistance in locating some archived material, along with our early conversations about what this project might look like, helped shape the direction of this book.

The challenge of writing such a personal story would not

have moved to completion without three people. Linda, my wife, has been a constant source of encouragement. Her observations and wise words proved crucial at significant points as I tried to put thoughts on paper.

Next, Barb Fuller's gracious words helped move the project forward at a time when I was on the verge of abandoning it. Thank you, Barb. What a rejoicing we will experience in heaven at long awaited reunions.

Lastly, I want to extend a deep appreciation to my editor, John Robin. The process of wrestling through edits brought portions of this work to life in ways I had not foreseen. Thank you for taking it on, for believing it was worth the energy, time, and conversation we put into it.

To all who have been part of my journey of faith, thank you.

Bibliography

Beaudette, J.N., J. Power, and L. Stewart. 2015. *National Prevalence of Mental Disorders among incoming Federally-Sentenced Men.* Research Report, Otttawa: Correctional Service of Canada.

Blaney, Leigh S. 2009. "Beyond 'knee jerk' reaction: CISM as a health promotion construct." *Irish Journal of Psychology* 37-57.

Bodkin, Claire, Lucie Pivnick, Susan J. Bondy, Carolyn Ziegler, Ruth Elwood Martin, Carey Jernigan, and Fiona Kouyoumdjian. 2019. "History of Childhood Abuse in Populations Incarcerated in Canada: A Systematic Review and Meta-Analysis." *American Journal of Public Health* 1-11.

Boin, Arjen, and William A. R. Rattray. 2004. "Understanding prison riots: Towards a threshold theory." *Punishment and Society* 47-65.

Canada, Correctional Service of. 2015. *Forum on Corrections Research.* 03 05. Accessed February 8, 2020. https://www.csc-scc.gc.ca/research/forum/e133/e133c-eng.shtml.

Canadian Baptist Federation. 1984. *A Manual for Worship and Service.* Toronto: All-Canada Baptist Publications.

Carter, Rod. 1996. "Days of Diamonds, Days of Stone." *The United Church Observer*, September: 29-30.

De Becker, Gavin. 1997. *The Gift of Fear: Survival Signals That Protect Us From Violence.* New York: Dell Publishing.

Edwards, Tilden. 1980. *Spiritual Friend.* New York: Paulist Press.

Erikson, Millard J. 1990. *Christian Theology.* Grand Rapids: Baker Book House.

Gladwell, Malcolm. 2019. *Talking to Strangers: What We Should Know About the People We Don't Know.* New York: Little, Brown and Company.

Humphreys, Keith, and Elizabeth Gifford. 2006. "Religion, Spirituality, and the Troublesome Use of Substances." In *Rethinking Substance Abuse: What Science Shows, and What we Should do about it*, by William R Miller and Kathleen M Carroll, 257-274. New York: The Guilford Press.

Johnson, Byron R. 2011. *More God Less Crime: Why Faith Matters and How it Could Matter More.* Conshohocken: Templton Press.

Maruna, Shadd, Louise Wilson, and Kathryn Curran. 2006. "Why God is Often Found Behind Bars: Prison Conversions and the Crisis of Self-Narrative." *Research in Human Development* 161-184.

Mate, Gabor. 2009. *In the Realm of Hungry Ghosts: Close Encounters with Addiction.* Toronto: Vintage Canada.

Smith, C. 2005. "Origin of Uses of Primum Non Nocere: Above All, Do Not Harm!" *Clincal Parmacology* 371-377.

Stoesz, Donald. 2020. *A Prison Chaplaincy Manual: The Canadian Context.* Victoria: Friesen Press.

Thompson, Francis. 1926. "The Project Gutenberg EBook of The Hound of Heaven." *Project Gutenberg.* Accessed February 18, 2020. https://www.gutenberg.org/files/30730/30730-h/30730-h.htm.

van Emmerik, A.A., J.H. Kamphuis, A.M. Hulsbosch, and P.M. Emmelkamp. 2002. "Single Session Debriefing after Psychological Trauma: A Meta-Analysis." *Lancet* 766-71.

Wenham, Gordon J. 1987. *Genesis 1-15: Word Biblical Commentary.* Edited by David A. Hubbard, Glenn W. Barker, and John D. Watts. Vol. 1. Waco, Texas: Word.

World Health Organization. 2019. *Burn-out an "occupational phenomenon": International Classification of Diseases.* May. Accessed December 28, 2020. https://www.who.int/news/item/28-05-2019-burn-out-an-occupational-phenomenon-international-classification-of-diseases.

About Hank Dixon

Hank Dixon, D.Min, is a retired minister and chaplain who has served Churches in Nova Scotia and worked in Canadian federal maximum, medium, and minimum security prisons. He has also been the Program Director of Open Circle, a Winnipeg-based prison visitation program. Over his years of involvement with corrections Hank has used his experiences as an inmate to help design chaplaincy course material along with training and supervising chaplains.

He lives in Winnipeg, Manitoba with Linda, his wife of 34 years. They have two grown children along with a beautiful granddaughter.